D0448807

LONGING

FOR A

HOMELAND

DISCOVERING the PLACE YOU BELONG

LONGING FOR A HOMELAND

DISCOVERING THE PLACE YOU BELONG

LYNN ANDERSON

FOREWORD BY LEE STROBEL

HOWARD
PUBLISHING CO

Our purpose at Howard Publishing is to:

• *Increase faith* in the hearts of growing Christians

• *Inspire holiness* in the lives of believers

• *Instill hope* in the hearts of struggling people everywhere

Because He's coming again!

Longing for a Homeland © 2004 by Lynn Anderson
All rights reserved. Printed in the United States of America
Published by Howard Publishing Co., Inc.
3117 North 7th Street, West Monroe, Louisiana 71291-2227
www.howardpublishing.com

04 05 06 07 08 09 10 11 12 13   10 9 8 7 6 5 4 3 2 1

Edited by Michele Buckingham
Interior design by John Mark Luke Designs and Gabe Cardinale
Cover design by Bill Chiaravalle, Brand Navigation, LLC

Anderson, Lynn, 1936-
   Longing for a homeland : discovering the place you belong / Lynn Anderson ; foreword by Lee Strobel.
      p. cm.
   ISBN 1-58229-353-8 (alk. paper)
   1. Home–Religious aspects–Christianity. I. Title.

BR115.H56A54 2004
248–dc22

                                                2003068555

No part of this publication may be reproduced in any form without the prior written permission of the publisher except in the case of brief quotations within critical articles and reviews.

Some of the names used in the stories in this book are not the actual names; identifying details have been changed to protect anonymity. Any resemblance is purely coincidental.

Scripture quotations not otherwise marked are from the HOLY BIBLE, NEW INTERNATIONAL VERSION©. Copyright © 1973, 1978, 1984 by International Bible Society. Used by permission of Zondervan. All rights reserved. Scripture quotations marked NLT are taken from the *Holy Bible,* New Living Translation, copyright © 1996. Used by permission of Tyndale House Publishers, Inc., Wheaton, Illinois 60189. All rights reserved. Scripture quotations marked NKJV are taken from The New King James Version. Copyright © 1982 by Thomas Nelson, Inc. Used by permission. All rights reserved. Scripture quotations marked MSG are taken from *THE MESSAGE.* Copyright © 1993, 1994, 1995, 1996. Used by permission of NavPress Publishing Group.

Italics in scripture have been added by the author for emphasis.

for Carolyn:

Thanks for walking home with me.

CONTENTS

CONTENTS

PART THREE:
I WANT TO GO HOME

PART FOUR:
IN ALL THE WRONG PLACES

PART FIVE:
HOMEWARD BOUND

PART SIX:
HOME AT LAST

FOREWORD

by Lee Strobel

I'm writing these words as my flight streaks across the sky toward my hometown of Chicago. I live in California now, and I always enjoy returning to the city where I grew up, worked as a journalist at the *Chicago Tribune,* and went from being an atheist to becoming a teaching pastor at a large church.

Even so, there's not much left of my childhood haunts. After my father died, the family sold the home in which I grew up. The first house that my wife and I ever bought has just been sold to a developer who plans to raze it and build a larger and more contemporary abode. Old neighbors have moved away. And today is a difficult journey. I'm returning to visit my mother, who's dying of cancer. If the doctors are right, she has only a short time to live.

My warm feelings about home, though, will inevitably live on even after her death. I suspect I will always be homesick for the place that continues to exist only in my memories. My heart will forever be tugged toward the neighborhood where my parents nurtured me and where my childhood unfolded.

Still, it's not surprising that my mother's illness has prompted thoughts about another home—a place that beckons us from beyond ourselves. This is the home I learned about when I shed my atheism and embraced Jesus. It's the home that offers hope to my mother. It's the home that's beyond death and sorrow. It's the place where our homesickness will be forever satisfied.

All of these thoughts percolated in my mind as I put down the manuscript for Lynn Anderson's new book, *Longing for a Homeland*. These themes of homesickness are developed with poignancy and power in the pages of this marvelous work. For me—and, I would guess, for you—this is a topic that resonates deeply.

Lynn is the ideal author to take on these matters. I first met Lynn several years ago when I was searching for a theologically attuned expert to discuss the haunting issue of doubt for my book *The Case for Faith*. Of the many Christian perspectives I have read on this topic, Lynn's perspective especially impressed me as being unvarnished in its honesty, sophisticated in its analysis, but most of all, always compassionate in its presentation.

My interview with Lynn exceeded all my expectations. He spoke eloquently about his own experiences with doubt, offered helpful insights, and encouraged others who were grappling with misgivings about their faith. Many have subsequently written to say how valuable Lynn's perspective has been to their own spiritual journey.

But what impressed me the most about Lynn was what happened before and after our interview. It was Lynn's gentle kindness, his gracious hospitality, his devotion to his wife and children, and his deep reservoir of wisdom that left an indelible impression on me.

Those same qualities are what make this book so meaningful. In the following pages, Lynn speaks from his heart about his rich lifetime of experiences—and through his stories, you'll come to understand more about your own situation. Through it all, Lynn's humanity and genuine caring will replenish and refresh you.

So, read on. Let Lynn take you on a journey to the kind of places that your heart has been longing for.

PREFACE

This book is for you . . .

- if you are homesick.
- if you are far, far away in a strange place.
- if you left home a long time ago and can't seem to get back.
- if you have no memories of a happy home, but you long to experience it someday.
- if you want to go home, but don't seem to know where home is.
- if your home has been broken by death or divorce or desertion—or just distance.
- if you are afraid to go home.
- if you once dreamed of creating a home, but your dreams were dashed.
- if you finally went back home, only to discover it isn't home anymore.
- if you can't stand the thought of going home.
- if . . .

ACKNOWLEDGMENTS

This book came together in wisps and fragments across a lifetime. However, I put the first draft down on paper the summer of 1988. Another draft in 1999. Some seasons I wrote furiously. At other times the unfinished chapters lay neglected for long spells. I guess I have been reluctant to finish the project—and have clung to it like a child I did not want to see leave home.

But publishers set deadlines. So, with twinges of grief, I now hug this book good-bye and send it out of my house.

I am indebted to many people who helped make it come together. Honorable mention goes to:

Michele, Debbie, Jon, and Christopher, my four grown children: You took time to read and suggest. And are willing to walk around in some of my stories.

Kay, Beverly, Audrey, and Margaret, my sisters: We called the old place our home.

Sam and Alice, dear friends for half a century: Thanks for lending me your house on Shushwap Lake in British Columbia, where I hid alone for six weeks and hammered out the first draft.

Phil and BJ, longtime friends and cheerleaders: You made possible my first writing sabbatical, which laid groundwork leading toward this book—and others.

Doc: Ol' buddy, you have traveled many a mile with me, including sentimental journeys across Canada and Sweden digging for my roots.

Carolyn, my soul mate, lover, and partner in ministry: You lived out most of these stories with me.

Jo Ann: You've been like a sister and this writer's constant cheerleader these thirty years.

Judy: You keyed in endless hours of edits, and you make everyone around you look more competent.

Allison: You chased footnotes through megamiles of cyberhighway and tirelessly retyped manuscript edits and permission requests—all with high professionalism and warm emotional ownership.

Michele Buckingham, editor for Howard Publishing Company: You turned the manuscript into an honest-to-goodness book. And you are so fun to work with.

All of you seemed to sense that this book means more to me than anything I have written so far. Thanks for the ride.

All died in faith, not having received the promises . . .
and confessed that they were strangers and pilgrims on
the earth. For those who say such things declare plainly
that they seek a homeland.

—Hebrews 11:13–14 NKJV

Home! Home! Sweet, sweet home!
There's no place like home.
No, there's no place like home!

—OLD AMERICAN FOLK SONG

When the child grew older, she took him to Pharaoh's
daughter and he became her son. She named him Moses,
saying, "I drew him out of the water."

—Exodus 2:10

A LONG LINE OF
WANDERERS

All of God's wanderers live—and die—homesick. In their earthly sojourns they are forever "looking for a country of their own" (Hebrews 11:14).

I think I belong to their tribe. I sometimes feel sentenced to endless homelessness, rootlessness.

The poet Walt Whitman wrote,

> *Facing west from California's shores . . .*
> *(But where is what I started for so long ago?*
> *And why is it yet unfound?)*[1]

Commenting on Whitman, Buckner Fanning writes, "We live on a planet of searchers. It's perpetual. From the crusaders, Sir Galahad searching for the Holy Grail, to Coronado searching for the Seven Cities of Cibola, Ponce de León searching for the Fountain of Youth. You're searching. We are all searching."[2]

What is this planet of searchers looking for?

I believe that, in one way or another, we are all longing for a homeland.

Strangers and Sojourners

Some of history's most significant homeland searchers have wandered through the pages of the Bible. Father Abraham was the first. God said, "Leave your country, your people and your father's household and go to the land I will show you" (Genesis 12:1). So Abraham left his home and began wandering the earth, "looking for a country of [his] own." He crisscrossed the Promised Land as a stranger and a sojourner; it never became his permanent place. Every few days Abraham packed up his black camelhair tent and moved on to a new campsite. In the end he died, never having settled in his homeland.

Hundreds of years later, Abraham's descendants wound up as slaves in Egypt. Landless. And homeless. There, in Egypt, the Bible's most famous wanderer was born. Though Moses lived a third of his lifetime like a prince in the splendor of an Egyptian palace, Egypt was not his home. For the next forty years, he lived as an exile in another strange land. Then, for his last forty years, he led his homeless, landless people through an alien wilderness.

Always a trespasser.

Always dodging some hostile clan.

Always longing for a homeland—yet never getting home.

Egypt wasn't home. Nor was Midian. The wilderness surely

wasn't. And if Canaan was home, Moses never got to go there. Wandering seemed to be his destiny. He was homeless all of his days.

Numerous people since have wandered many a wilderness, searching for, yearning for, a homeland. In the words of Scripture, "All these people were still living by faith when they died. They did not receive the things promised; they only saw them and welcomed them from a distance. And they admitted that they were aliens and strangers on earth. People who say such things show that they are looking for a country of their own" (Hebrews 11:13-14).

The Road Map

Everyone loves a story. So the following pages explore the geography of several home-longing stories: Moses longing for his own "promised land." European immigrants looking for a new homeland in America. First Nations peoples being driven brokenhearted from the homeland of their fathers. A prodigal son trying desperately to get back to the home he once knew. And through these pages I ponder my own story, my own wanderings, as I—like the prodigal—have tried to get back home.

In the chapters that follow, I will take you with me on my literal, physical wanderings—my "sentimental journeys." At times we will go back to the place of my childhood, to the Canadian homestead on which I was born. At other times we will go to Tennessee, where I met my wife, Carolyn, and began many other lifelong relationships. We'll go to British Columbia, where three of our children were born and where we helped plant two churches. And to Texas, where we have lived now these thirty-plus years.

You will join me on a rail trip I once took across Canada, from Quebec City to Vancouver, in an attempt to possess my Canadian homeland. Another time we will travel all the way to Sweden, the country of my paternal roots.

At times our journey will take us back into Canadian history, which I restudied as an adult in hopes of better understanding where I belong. It will take us into portions of American history. We'll revisit places and events that link together the First Nations people and the immigrants and my childhood homestead.

Mostly, however, I will take you with me on my internal searchings. We will wander through that inner "far country" that most of us carry around in our souls. There, as in all of our travels, our companion and guide will be Moses, the greatest of all wanderers, who always carried with him his longing for a homeplace, a home people—a homeland.

I spread my stories across these pages with the heartfelt prayer that somehow they will put a few pilgrims in touch with their homesickness. Perhaps encourage others to embrace their natural longing for a homeland. Maybe help a few more take the first step on a journey home.

There are obvious differences between the many stories we're about to explore, yet a common thread is woven through them all. Moses and the Israelites, the European immigrants, the First Nations people, my ancestors, me, you: All of us are wanderers.

A note of explanation: The terms "First Nations peoples" and "First Nations people" are used throughout the book to refer to Native Americans and Native Canadians. We chose these terms in an effort to be respectful and inclusive of the proud people who first called this continent their homeland.

I invite you, my homesick friend, to turn the page and wander with me through far-off countries as we share our longing for a homeland. Perhaps together we will find our way home.

PART ONE

HOMESICK

I could not quiet that pearly ache in my heart
that I diagnosed as the cry of home.

—PAT CONROY

I listen to someone who begins with a confession of thirst, of homesickness.

—PHILIP YANCEY

CHAPTER ONE

I WANT TO GO HOME

Carolyn and I have four children—two girls, then two boys—who all tend to reflect their blond-haired, blue-eyed Swedish genes. Our oldest son, Jon, married Joanna, whose maiden name was Gomez. Of course, you wouldn't expect Joanna to look like the rest of the Andersons. She is a strikingly beautiful Hispanic woman and a delight to our lives.

Jon and Joanna's first child, Abby, was born with nearly blond hair and nearly blue eyes (leading her *abuelo*—"grandfather"—on the Gomez side to wonder if the wrong baby might have been brought home from the hospital!). Then Abby's brother, Connor, was born. He sports a full head of copper-red hair, a color that resembles neither side of the family.

When the third child was due, I asked Abby, "Do you want a brother or a sister?"

"Oh, Pappy," she answered, "I want a sister."

"And Connor," I queried, "what do *you* want?"

Quick as a flash he responded, "I want a *Mexican!*"

When Ana was born, they both got their wish. Abby got her sister. Connor got his Mexican. Ana has jet-black hair and olive skin. She is as charming as her mother and as gregarious as her abuelo, Bob Gomez.

When Ana was four, Jon and Joanna accompanied Carolyn and me on a trip to Israel. Ana, Abby, and Connor were left in the charge of Aunt Michele and Uncle Wes. Now, two weeks away from parents is a long time for a four-year-old child. Ana fared pretty well, aided by a photograph of Mommy and Daddy that she could look at any time she wanted. But on one of those final few days, Uncle Wes corrected Ana for some small mischief. Her lower lip poked out, and she ran up the stairs to her room. Concerned that he had been too tough, Wes slipped up the stairs and peeked in on her. She was sitting in the middle of the bed, holding the picture of Mommy and Daddy tightly in both hands, salt trails sliding down both cheeks, fighting back sobs.

She finally noticed her uncle peeking through the door. "Uncle Wes," Ana announced in a forlorn, but deliberate, tone, "I think I want to go home now!"

Me too, Ana. Home. I want to go home!

The Meaning of Home

Galaxies of emotion cluster around this little word, *home*. For most of us, home means warm and welcome feelings: thoughts of parents, brothers and sisters, holidays, coming in from school, Sunday dinners, birthdays, Christmas mornings, summer vacations.

Warm memories. Fond dreams. Home!

For others of us, however, the word *home* triggers hidden pain. We remember neglect. Alienation. Separation. Abuse. Rejection.

One morning as I huddled with staff members to plan a special Mother's Day service at our church, talk drifted nostalgically toward memories of our mothers. One person in the circle listened quietly for nearly ten minutes, then suddenly exploded, "I can't do this! I dread Mother's Day. I hated home, and I don't have any pleasant memories about my mother." He added, "My wife feels the same way about her mother. My hunch is that a huge bunch of folks are going to be sitting out there feeling a lot like us."

How incredibly disturbing. And true. Yet the magnitude of the pain only confirms the huge space that home-hunger occupies among our deepest longings. No matter what our emotional history, we all want to feel at home. Somewhere. Somehow.

A Universal Longing

Most of my life, both by vocation and by passion, I have studied people. And in the process, I have come to believe that all of us are homesick. In fact, our innate home-longing seems to serve as a sort of universal frame of reference for us:

A *fugitive* is one who is running away from home.

A *vagabond* is one who has no home.

A *refugee* is one who has been driven from home.

A *stranger* is one who is away from home.

A *pilgrim* is one who is on the way home.

A *divorcée* or *divorcé* is one who has lost his or her home.

This universal homing instinct creeps into the most unexpected places—even old nursery rhymes:

> *Little Bo Peep has lost her sheep,*
> *And can't tell where to find them;*
> *Leave them alone and they'll come home,*
> *Wagging their tails behind them.*

Don't worry, Bo Peep, they'll be back. The magnet of home will draw them. And they'll wag their little, woolly banners of joy to celebrate their happy homecoming.

The two strands of that old rhyme—the tug of home and the joy of coming home—are inextricably woven into the fabric of all human longing. Ah, yes. For some the word *home* means warmth. For others it means mostly pain. For still others, the word reawakens feelings of disappointed frustration; home is that illusive *something* they have longed for all their lives but have never found. Some have even lost hope that they will ever experience it.

However we define it, we all long for home. And we all carry with us our picture of home—whether real or imagined—wherever we go.

Polka music is all about longing for your homeland.

—**FRANKIE YANKOVIC**

Hear my prayer, O LORD, *listen to my cry*

for help; be not deaf to my weeping.

For I dwell with you as an alien,

a stranger, as all my fathers were.

—PSALM 39:12

CHAPTER TWO

THE IMMIGRANTS:
A HOMELAND FOUND

One whole windy autumn day, I roamed the wharfs and halls of Ellis Island in New York City. To millions of immigrants from the far-flung corners of the globe, this was the doorway to America at the dawn of the twentieth century.

The American Immigrant Wall of Honor that encircles the island's museum bears more than 500,000 names. Yet, as the tourist brochure notes, those immigrants passed through the gates of Ellis Island "one at a time, individual by individual."[1] Real people. Maybe my ancestors, both maternal and paternal. Possibly your ancestors too.

My journal entry at Ellis Island reminds me of the way that place whispered to my soul:

New York City, November 1997

I move almost reverently through this place, communing with the ghosts of those who passed through here in yesteryears. Wearing quaint clothing. Speaking strange languages. The noise of my footsteps echoing through these vast halls makes me wonder if the clatter of immigrant shoes on hard floors long ago signaled a confidence not actually felt by the frightened folks who wore them.

A wall placard explains, "Most immigrants came to America in search of a better life ... free from oppression." But many came "longing for some land of their own that they could call home."

Some immigrants paid an enormous price. Passage from Europe to America cost only thirty dollars, if you rode steerage class. But steerage usually meant being dumped into the bowels of the ship to live for weeks like animals in dark, cramped conditions.[2] The passengers often slept in heaps, ate meager rations of rotting food, and were smothered in stench and disease. A wall placard at Ellis Island quotes one immigrant mother of several children who said: "It was so miserable, I prayed the ship would go down." And in fact, the mortality rate among the steerage passengers was approximately 10 percent per voyage.

When they finally landed—the ground still swaying like waves beneath their feet, the shrill shouts of a dozen different languages assaulting their ears—they were processed like cattle, as many as twelve thousand per day.[3] Another placard puts it this way: "They gave up everything. Their families. Their friends. Their homes. The villages they were born in. They arrived with only the clothes on their backs. Vulnerable. Scared. And most of them knew they could not ever go home again. Yet they were brimming with hope and determined that a better life was within their grasp."

They Are Us

Some time ago the *Arkansas Democrat Gazette* stated that "forty percent of all Americans can trace their ancestry to someone who registered at Ellis Island. Their history is our history. Their lives have become our lives. The Ellis Island Immigration Museum teaches us not only about the people pictured and quoted there, but also about ourselves."[4]

In other words, *the immigrants are us.*

While I am not sure of the arrival dates of my Swedish paternal ancestors nor of my German maternal ones, I do know they came to the United States first and then later migrated to Canada. My visit to Ellis Island conjured up a collage of possible scenarios surrounding them. I can only imagine what they really experienced.

My paternal great-grandfather, Per Erik Anderson, came from Sweden to America alone. Once he got work and saved enough money, he brought Carolina, my great-grandmother, and their two children to the lumber camps of Minnesota. Their financial situation being what it was, they surely must have crossed the Atlantic in steerage class. On the final leg of the journey up the St. Croix River, there was only enough ticket money for Carolina and the children to take a boat; so Per Erik followed on foot, walking along the riverbank.

I know much less about my maternal great-grandparents and their arrival from Germany, but very likely their experience was not much different from that of Per Erik and Carolina. They too came looking for a new homeland.

A Common Longing

For four centuries now, immigrants have streamed to this continent. Not all have come to America by choice. Thousands were brought from Africa by force, torn from their homelands. Forced into slavery. They shuffled around the South, their family members treated like dispensable and interchangeable parts. Today their descendants call America "home," but many struggle with feeling fully at home.

During the last half-century, more people than ever have come to America from more places than ever. Large numbers have come from Asia. The Middle East. Latin America. We can only guess what forces conspired to bring this family or that—this ethnic group or that—to these shores. We can be certain, however, that whether they came by choice or by coercion, all had one thing in common: *home-longing.* All were either losing or seeking a sense of home.

I'm reminded of a conversation in Johan Bojer's classic novel, *The Emigrants:*

"Are you a newcomer here?"

"Oh no, not at all! I first came over from Norway forty years ago."

"You don't say so! And you took a trip home last year?"

"I have been back to Norway seven times."

"That's something to boast of!"

"And each time I thought I was going back for good. *Now I'll settle down*, I thought. But happiness is a funny thing! When you're here, you feel you can't be happy out of the old country, and when you've been there a little while, you begin to look out across the ocean, and you find that you're happier over there, after all!"

The old man smiled mournfully; there was a faraway look in his eyes, as though they were always gazing across an ocean.[5]

Home is that place from which,

when a man has departed,

he is a wanderer until he returns.

—SIR WILLIAM BLACKSTONE

CHAPTER THREE

THE OUT-WANDERERS

Home-longing seems imprinted in the human DNA. We so hunger for a place to belong. Some of us search a lifetime for that elusive permanent abode, that land of our own. Others of us feel as if we were "at home" once long ago, and now we're trying to get back there—but we can't seem to find our way.

At least I feel like this. Most of my life I have felt somewhat homesick for somewhere, and yet I have never been able to figure out exactly where that somewhere is. Lee Marvin sang my theme song:

> I was born under a wand'rin' star
> Achin' for to stop and always achin' for to go;
> Searchin', but for what I never will know.
> I was born under a wand'rin' star.[1]

Redigging My Roots

This restless longing may actually have come to me from my father and to him from his father, which Granddad in turn got from my great-granddad. For generations the men in my lineage, both paternal and maternal, have been wanderers—searching, I think, for a homeland.

One memorable evening a few years back, I boarded an overnight boat leaving Turku, Finland, for Stockholm, Sweden. After dinner I watched the sun set over the North Sea, then hit my bunk and dreamed of an ancestral homeland. The next day, up before dawn, I went out on the deck and peered into the half-light. I couldn't wait to see the land of my paternal roots— the land my grandfather knew as home for the first five years of his life. As the sun rose, I leaned on the ship's rail, feeling a tsunami of emotion as the colorful sights of Stockholm slipped in around me. My journal remembers that morning:

Stockholm, Sweden, June 13, 2000

This may be one of the best days of my life, and I do feel as if— as John Denver sang it—I'm "coming home to a place I'd never been before": Stockholm, Sweden. Key city of the land of my paternal ancestors. Just after sunrise this morning, we sail into the harbor. At many coastal cities, you sail up to the city port. But you sail into Stockholm, where the harbor lies at the very heart of the city. One of the more impressive sights of my life! Cathedral spires stabbing the morning sky. Some new buildings, like the Ericsson Telephone headquarters. Plenty of older structures. White huvillas with red roofs. Some with green roofs and yellow walls. A smorgasbord of visual delight! Can hardly believe my good fortune as I try to absorb this—my eyes are actually feasting on Sweden.

The next day my friends David and Joseph and I, guided by our new Swedish friend Terttu, drove inland to the picturesque country parish of Fellingsbro, where Grandpa Eric's birth is registered. Saint Ansgar evangelized Vikings here in the ninth century. A thirteenth-century tower beside the church claims to be the "oldest church fortress in central Sweden." Inside the church I laid my hand on the shiny lip of the baptismal font (here since the fourteenth century) where Grandpa Eric was christened 133 years ago.

Afterward we left Fellingsbro and drove fifteen miles to Vastra Skedv, where I found the baptismal place of my great-grandfather, Per Erik. And in an old cemetery there, I may have discovered the gravestone of my great-great-grandfather: Ander's Son.

Redigging my Swedish roots proved to be a rich, unforgettable, once-in-a-lifetime experience. I'm glad I did it. But it didn't get me *home*, as I might have hoped. On the contrary, it put me more in touch with a wanderer's homesickness. On the drive back to Stockholm, Terttu taught me a new Swedish word: *utvandrarna*, which means the "out-wanderers" or "those who wander away." Locals used this word in the nineteenth century to describe their neighbors who left Sweden for the New World.

Utvandrarna seems to have been bred into the bones of my forefathers. Mine too.

The Homesteaders

My great-grandfather, Per Erik Anderson, came to America from Sweden in the 1870s. Class prejudice may have been the trigger. My great-great-grandfather, a Swedish landowner, disinherited Per Erik because Per would not give up his romance with a peasant girl, the milkmaid, Carolina. So Per Erik found himself landless and homeless in Sweden. And when he heard rumors of free land in America, he headed alone across a wide ocean looking for a new homeland, eventually bringing his Carolina and their two young children to Wisconsin. One of these children was my Grandpa Eric, just five years old when he left Sweden.

By the time he was grown, Grandpa Eric was also infected with wanderlust. After my grandmother, Anna, died of the flu following the birth of her fifth child, Grandpa Eric took his young family and migrated northwest to Saskatchewan, Canada, to search for land of his own. The year was 1913. My father was just a lad of eight.

Grandpa Eric homesteaded virgin land—mostly barren, rocky hills—on one of the last frontiers in usable North America, just north of the Montana border. Kal, a character in Johan Bojer's *The Emigrants*, helps me imagine the strange thrill my grandfather must have felt the day his plow first broke the virgin sod that had lain undisturbed for thousands of years:

> Kal had yoked the oxen to the plow before daybreak, and when the sun began to lift its golden rim above the plain, he stood there ready and waiting. Now he could start plowing . . . breaking up prairie land till the sweat fairly rained off him. A dark-brown wave was rolling up behind him. . . . Turning the plow, he began another furrow. As the soil curled over, it gleamed in the morning sunlight. For thousands of years this soil had lain here waiting for him, and now he had come.[2]

Both Grandpa Eric and Dad called this land "the homeplace." Later I would too. In reality, of course, Dad and Grandpa were not the first to live on the homeplace, nor were they the last. First Nations peoples had called the land "home" for centuries, up until a few short years before my family arrived. Other families eventually followed ours.

Once my father was grown, a new restlessness prompted Grandpa to move to a fresh homestead further north, leaving my dad on the original south Saskatchewan land. Later, after Grandpa turned seventy-five, he let the northern homestead go and came back to live with us for a while. Then he spent his last few years in a retirement home. By the time Grandpa died, he was once again landless and homeless.

My Childhood Home

My maternal grandfather, Henry Theis, came to Wisconsin from Luxemburg in the 1870s, around the same time Per Erik Anderson arrived from Sweden. Later Grandpa Theis immigrated to western Canada, homesteading first at Leduc, Alberta. Still later he moved by oxcart to Kincaid, Saskatchewan. Always moving. Searching. Longing.

When my mom and dad, the children of pioneers, married, they remained for some years on the land homesteaded by my paternal grandfather. Dad broke still more of the virgin prairie. I can remember seeing Dad's plow turn the ancient sod dark-side-up in fresh, first-time furrows, his eyes filled with sheer joy—the same joy, I can only imagine, that lit up the eyes of my grandpa decades earlier.

During my childhood years, I felt that place would be my home forever. I roamed that homestead, explored every square yard of it. I knew every coulee and every hill. Knew which chokecherry bushes yielded the sweetest fruit. Which spots were best for snaring jack rabbits. I could take you to the draw where the most colorful crocuses exploded from the soil each spring. The exact wrinkle in the prairie hillside where the coyote pup-birthing den was hidden. The brush patch where hawks nested year after year.

Often I would stand on the big hill a mile southwest of our house and look out over "our land." On dark winter evenings, I would follow Dad to the barn, carrying the lantern as the hard, cold snow crunched under our feet. Dad would point to the glistening crystals at the edges of that pool of lantern glow and say, "Look—we are rich. God has covered our land with diamonds."

I loved the daily, two-and-a-half-mile adventure walk to Pebble Hill, our one-room country schoolhouse. But then the school closed in my seventh-grade year, and I switched to riding horseback to neighboring Patriotic School five miles away. Some evenings, riding home through the gathering winter darkness on the back of Old Bird, my swift black mare, I found myself singing an old folk song my dad used to sing:

> *Seven hills to home,*
> *Seven hills to home,*
> *Though the way was full of hardships*
> *As o'er those hills we'd roam*
> *I'm always looking forward to*
> *Those seven hills to home.*

Seemed like that song was written for Old Bird and me, because I could count exactly seven hills between the Patriotic schoolhouse and our old homeplace.

Leaving Home

Although my father tended his land for more than thirty years, in retrospect I wonder if he ever felt completely at home there. Dad loved that land all right, but it was not a permanent dwelling place to him. He held it lightly and for only a few short decades, then left it to move on to other things.

I also left that land—much too young. Since no high school was nearby, the folks sent me away to boarding school when I was fourteen years old. The day I left, Dad drove me and my old, scuffed cardboard suitcase twelve dirt-road miles to the little village of McCord to catch the eastbound morning train. He set the case on the platform, then stood quietly and looked at me a long time. He shook my hand. Then cleared his throat. Then squeezed my shoulders with a hug. Then shook my hand again. He kept repeating these motions and blinking back tears, his twitching lips unable to form words.

Finally he spoke huskily and abruptly: "Be strong, Son. And—and remember who you are." Then he turned on his heel and strode resolutely to the car. As the train pulled out of the station, I could see Dad standing by the old Pontiac, watching me leave his life.

As the coach rattled down the tracks, I tried to weep out the big lump in my throat. Somehow I knew I would never live at home again. Oh yes, I returned briefly over a few summers and blew through for short visits. But I never really went "back home." I never have.

By the time Mom and Dad died, the old homeplace had long since passed into the possession of others, some of whom are strangers to me. And actually, in those last years of his life—especially the last few months—Dad made it clear that he wanted out of this world. No, he wasn't depressed. It was just that people and places had drifted into the past. Family had scattered. Old friends were gone. After he carried Mom to the cemetery, not much held Dad here. He was still longing for a homeland.

Sometimes in my own nostalgic home-longings, I wish I could bring back a few more of those childhood years with Mom and Dad. I wish I had "our land" in my "possession" again. Whenever bittersweet memories flicker in my soul, I go back to rewalk those hills, trying to recapture the at-home feelings of my youth. But in my heart I know that place is no longer my home. Hasn't been for fifty years. In some ways, I think, *it never really was.*

Joe Diffie sang my feelings for me:

> *The only thing I see ahead is just the heat*
> *a risin' on the road,*
> *The rainbows I've been chasin' keep on fading,*
> *before I find my pot of gold.*
> *And more and more I'm thinking, that the only*
> *treasures that I'll ever know,*
> *Are long ago and far behind wrapped up in my*
> *memories of home.*
> *Home was a swimming hole, and a fishing pole,*
> *And the feel of a muddy road between my toes.*

PART ONE: HOMESICK

Home was a back porch swing where I would

sit and mama'd sing

Amazing Grace, while she hung out the clothes.

Home is an easy chair, with my daddy there

And the smell of Sunday supper on the stove.

My footsteps carry me away,

But in my mind I'm always going home.[3]

Never thought my heart could be so yearny.

Why did I decide to roam?

Gotta take that sentimental journey,

Sentimental journey home.

—BUD GREEN, LES BROWN, AND BEN HOMER

CHAPTER FOUR

SENTIMENTAL JOURNEY

In the summer of 1994, I took a "sentimental journey" across Canada by rail, accompanied by an old friend. On the train I encountered dozens of other people taking sentimental journeys of their own. Peek over my shoulder into a page of my journal:

Aboard the VIA Trans-Canadian train, Sioux Lookout, Ontario
August 28, 1994

> *I board the VIA in Quebec City bound all the way across Canada, past Toronto, across the prairies, and then through the Rockies to Vancouver. This is my first time to cross my entire homeland. I have read of Eastern Canada all my life, knowing that it is part of "my own, my native land" (as Sir Walter Scott wrote). Now, as I begin my trip, I am experiencing it. But am I exploring my homeland? Or am I actually "trying to get home"?*
>
> *And what of the other people on this train? Mike from Alberta is traveling with his son, Andy. Mike tells me he is Ukrainian by race, Polish by birth. His family was in the last*

shipload of immigrants to leave Poland before World War II broke out. The Nazi war machine was heating up, so Mike's father, along with thousands of other people, decided to flee Poland and sail for Canada. Mike recalls leaving Europe aboard the sailing vessel Athenia as a small child in 1939. He and his family were refugees, yet they felt excited about finding a new homeland.

But just one day out to sea, Mike heard a whump as the torpedoes from German U-boats struck the Athenia. He felt the ship shudder before the lights went out. It was bedtime, so most passengers were in their nightclothes. Mike's father quickly dressed his family, preparing for the worst—which soon came. The Athenia, carrying twelve hundred passengers, sank that night. One hundred twenty people perished. Sixty when a lifeboat became entangled and dumped its occupants into the icy brine. Sixty more when another lifeboat drifted into the ship's propellers.

After more than twenty-four hours on the open sea, the survivors were rescued by a Norwegian freighter and taken to Scotland. Terrified of boarding another ship, Mike's family tried to go back to Poland. But it was too late. War had closed that door, and the Polish government advised the whole group to find another ship to Canada. They could never go back home again.

The second ship bore Mike's family safely across to Canada. Then a rail train took them two thousand miles west to Vegreville, Alberta, where Mike's father paid ten dollars for 160 acres of land far back from the railroad. The former owner hauled the immigrants by wagon to their new home and dropped them off. Mike recounts, "So this was my father's new homeland, far from neighbors, with only a suitcase, a shovel, and an ax—and a wife and three children—and only one short summer to prepare for a long winter."

These hardy Ukrainian immigrants survived that first winter and, in time, built a prosperous farm. Later Mike became successful in the construction business in Edmonton. He is now retired, and for the first time—like me—he is exploring his homeland.

Over the days that followed, I talked with many people riding the cross-country train. Conversation after conversation convinced me that Mike and I were not alone. Most of the passengers were searching—consciously or not—for a deeper sense of home.

Maternal Roots

At various points on my sentimental journey, my friend and I left the train to explore some of the back roads of my homeland. Again, my journal speaks:

Kincaid, Saskatchewan, August 29, 1994

At Saskatoon we leave the train, rent a four-wheel-drive vehicle, and head south across the prairies to Kincaid, Saskatchewan. My maternal grandfather, Henry Theis, who spoke only German during his life, migrated from Wisconsin to Canada, home-steading at Leduc, Alberta. But dry summers and brutal winters drove him from that dream. So he loaded my grandmother, Margaret, and their family into an ox-drawn wagon and moved five hundred miles southeast to a new piece of prairie near Kincaid. My mother lived out her childhood in Kincaid, about forty miles from my paternal Grandpa Eric's homestead.

Years later, in September 1936, Kincaid was the place where I first saw the light of day. Now I am bent on exploring the area, especially the old Theis homeplace. Since it has been out of Mom's family since I was a small child, I hold only vague memories of it.

At the Kincaid post office, I learn that Janet, my niece by marriage, just happens to be in town. What is more, I am surprised to learn that Janet's in-laws now farm the Theis land. So this evening, Janet guides our nostalgic tour of the Theis home-place.

As we pull off the gravel road into the yard, long-slumbering memories stir to life. I actually recognize the two original build-ings still bravely standing watch over the fading past. One is an outbuilding (with its peculiar, curved, half-moon roof) that was once Grandpa Theis's blacksmith shop. The other is the old two-story house, dilapidated but still fairly intact. On one partly plas-tered attic wall, I find Xs and Os still clearly visible. My mother once told me that she and her sisters had scribbled them there, now more than eighty years ago.

Ghosts of my ancestors haunt this house. And while I do feel a mysterious connection with this place, I feel no sense of home here. In fact, revisiting these relics of my mother's roots makes me feel even more homeless and only sharpens my hunger for a homeland.

Moses, my friend, I can't help but wonder: When you went back to Egypt after forty years to walk once more through Pharaoh's palaces, did you see old wall scratchings left there by your childhood hand? What old memories did they stir? One thing I'm sure of, Moses: Long-ago scenes rising up in your memory may have brought tears, but they didn't make you feel at home in Egypt.

Egypt was never your home.

PART TWO

INVISIBLE WINDS, IRRESISTIBLE FORCES

The old order changeth, yielding place to new,
and God fulfills Himself in many ways.

—ALFRED, LORD TENNYSON

Moses fled from Pharaoh and went to live in Midian,

where he sat down by a well.

—EXODUS 2:15

CHAPTER FIVE

THE FIRST NATIONS PEOPLE: A HOMELAND LOST

From a shelf in my Texas hill-country study, the top half of a grayish-white buffalo skull stares down at me day after day. I wish it could tell its story. If it could, that skull might tell of its strange connection with a boy of eleven, a sixty-six-year-old man, and several circles of stones. Both the boy and the man would be me. And the stones . . . ?

Wander over the hills I roamed as a child, and on the ridge southwest of the old house, you might stumble onto several circles of milk-carton-sized stones half hidden in the prairie grass. The stones lie arranged in a large circle of small circles. Each of the smaller circles marks the spot where a tepee once stood, its edges weighted down with stones against the strong prairie winds.

Short decades before my grandfather homesteaded the place, First Nations families camped here. Local historians suggest that a few of the circles may have been left by none other than Chief Sitting Bull and his people during their four years in Canada, where they fled in the aftermath of the Battle of the Little Big Horn.

Sitting Bull entered Canada near Val Marie, about forty-five miles west of our old homeplace. I actually have some of the journals of his negotiations with the Royal Northwest Mounted Police while he was in the vicinity of Wood Mountain, Saskatchewan, only about twenty miles east from my childhood home.[1] This means that during their time in Canada, Sitting Bull and his warriors roamed through the very vicinity of the stone tepee circles that dot not only our old homestead but also many of the neighboring ranches.

Talking Bones

As a child I often cut across pastureland on my way home from school. On one of those days, I discovered in a marshy coulee at the foot of a sharp bluff the bones of dozens of buffalo—a "buffalo jump"—scarcely two miles from our house. I was eleven, and the bones, bleached white by the sun, seemed ancient to me then, although they could not have lain in that spot much more than sixty or seventy years. I found several buffalo skulls that day, including one so complete that part of the hulls still clung to the horns.

Fifty years after that childhood discovery, in the summer of 1998, I returned to that same marshy coulee, wondering if any buffalo bones still remained. Nearly an hour of searching turned up nothing. It seemed all the bones had vanished—

carried away by curious boys or buried deep under the marsh by fifty years of stomping cattle hooves.

I was about to leave when I spotted a bone fragment peering up from under a tuft of grass. After a few tugs, out came the buffalo skull that now rests on my shelf.

Do the math: It took fifty years of stomping cattle to bury those bones, which had probably rested there for sixty or seventy years before I found them as a boy. Which means the buffalo could have been killed between 1876 and 1881, when Sitting Bull and his warriors roamed those very hills. It is at least technically possible that the buffalo skull on my shelf was killed by the hunting party of none other than Sitting Bull himself!

Of course, this is only speculation, but I like to imagine my buffalo skull actually marked the location of one of Sitting Bull's hunts—and that some of those rock circles on the hills near my childhood home mark one of his camps. But whether Sitting Bull was there or not, one thing is sure: Real, live, warm-blooded First Nations families lived on that ridge not too many years before I was born.

But then their homeland was taken from them.

And the next people to claim the land were my father and my grandfather, who homesteaded the place in 1913—scarcely thirty-two years after Sitting Bull passed through.

This place I called home, that I still love to walk on and smell and touch, was actually taken from people who walked on it, smelled it, touched it, and called it home long before I did. I can't help but feel a twinge of guilt. I sometimes wonder if my father might have felt it too.

Invisible Winds

The larger forces that shape and drive the universe are invisible to the human eye. Gravity grips us to the globe and glues the galaxies together. Invisible winds shape the weather patterns and thus the contours and the food sources of the planet. Electricity drives economies and turns night to day. Love and sacrifice, although invisible, build nations. Hate and greed rip them apart.

All these forces, while unseen, are immensely powerful and history shaping. Just so, the invisible longing for a homeland drives the wheels of progress toward broad new horizons and fuels the search for fresh continents—on the one hand. On the other hand, home-longing has its devastating downsides.

And so it has been for millennia. The characters have changed, but the plot has remained essentially the same as this drama has played out on many a stage across the human epic. Under the invisible but relentless force of home-longing, humankind has wandered the earth. Heading for this homeland. Driving others from that homeland. Staying for a season. Or for centuries. But never permanently.

When one people gains a homeland, it seems another people loses one. Even Joshua, when he led the Israelites into their Promised Land, drove native peoples from their ancestral homes through bloody and violent conquests. Homeland dis-putes between Jews and Arabs still rage across the Middle East hundreds of generations later, just as violent today as they ever were. Even as I write, television newscasters tell of escalating horror as Jews and Palestinians seek to drive each other from what both claim as their homeland. Short years ago we watched the bloodbath in Kosovo, as Serbs attempted to drive Albanian Kosovars from their land. Before that, it was the Hutus and Tutsis and near-genocide in Rwanda. Before that, Northern Ireland. And before that . . .

Irresistible Forces

It happened in "civilized" North America too. The hunger for a homeland that brought Grandpa Eric and Grandpa Theis and millions of immigrants to North America drove millions of native people—the First Nations—from the homelands they knew and loved. To the immigrants, this vast, untamed country was a new homeland for the taking. But to the First Nations, this land had long been home.

At first the native people seemed to hope there was land enough for everybody, natives and immigrants alike. But the whites kept coming in numbers unimaginable to the First Nations peoples, and there wasn't room for all.

Over several decades the immigrants broke treaties, changed boundaries, and whittled away at the land of the First Nations, leaving for reservations only what surveyors believed to be worthless. The Black Hills of South Dakota, for example, were specifically left to the native people by treaty. To the whites, they were worthless. To the First Nations peoples, they were sacred. But as soon as General George Armstrong Custer reported that the Black Hills were filled with gold, the whites ignored the treaty and swarmed the region.

The First Nations people lost not only their land but their livelihood as well. The buffalo was a main staple of their life. But then General Philip H. Sheridan gave this order to his troops: "Kill, skin, and sell until the buffalo is exterminated, as it is the only way to bring lasting peace and allow civilization to advance."[2] As the buffalo were systematically slaughtered, the governments of the United States and Canada herded the First Nations people onto reservations. Sadly, only a fraction of the supplies promised by the two governments actually reached most reservations. Consequently, malnutrition and disease killed off thousands of men, women, and children like flies.

Some First Nations peoples would not submit to reservation life, however. The U.S. military referred to these as "hostiles." And one of the most powerful leaders among the hostiles was Ta-tan'ka I-yo-ta'ke.

Better known as Chief Sitting Bull.

The proud warrior who may have lived and hunted on the land I grew up calling "home."

Even now I look up at the buffalo skull on my shelf, and I remember.

By the rivers of Babylon we sat and wept

when we remembered Zion. . . .

How can we sing the songs of the LORD

while in a foreign land?

—PSALM 137:1-4

CHAPTER SIX

RUNNING FOR HOME

While the First Nations people on the reservations suffered enormously, most who stayed away from reservation life survived reasonably well at first. Then a government edict in December 1875 ordered all the "hostiles" to return to the reservations at once—by January 31, 1876.[1]

Runners went out from the various Western agencies to warn the free chiefs to come into the reservations, but blizzards kept the couriers from getting through until weeks after the January 31 deadline. However, even if Sitting Bull and the other chiefs had gotten word and wanted to comply, they could not have been expected to move their women and children in such weather. The January 31 deadline was unrealistic, and the chiefs didn't take it seriously.

Consequently, in February 1876, the U.S. War Department authorized General Philip Henry Sheridan to commence operations against the "hostile Sioux"; and as historian Dee Brown observes, "Once this machinery of government began moving, it became an inexorable force, mindless and uncontrollable."[2] On March 17, without warning, the military attacked the camp of a mixed band of hungry First Nations families who were sleeping along the Powder River in southeastern Montana. The cavalry Blue Coats burned tepees, food, and saddles and drove away over twelve hundred horses.

This action pushed otherwise peaceful First Nations peoples into a fighting mood. Several Sioux chiefs, led by Chief Sitting Bull of the Hunkpapa tribe, moved north and west in search of game and grass. Along the way, more bands of Lakota Sioux joined them: Brule, Sans Arc, Blackfoot, Miniconjou, and Cheyenne. By the time they reached the Rosebud River, the combined Sioux camp had swelled to several thousand.

On June 17, 1876, General George Crook and his soldiers tried to arrest the whole camp, but the sheer numbers and skill of the Sioux warriors whipped Crook into retreat. This failure prompted Crook to call for reinforcements. The chiefs, meanwhile, feeling more bold and secure, moved further west to the valley of the Little Bighorn, following reports of antelope herds and plenty of green grass.

More tribes continued to flock to the safety of numbers, and the camp grew to stretch some three miles along the river. The people dined daily on antelope and wild turnips. At night they held tribal dances.

Then suddenly, on the morning of June 25, 1876, their peace was permanently shattered.

Little Big Horn

The reinforcements arrived. Major Marcus Reno and his soldiers attacked from the south, smashing tepees and running down women and children in a wild melee. The tribal warriors quickly forced Reno back across the Little Big Horn River into the hills, but not before many in the camp had been killed.

Minutes later General George Armstrong Custer's army moved in from the hills to attack from the north. Hundreds of Sioux warriors splashed through the river and stormed up the hillsides and ravines in counterattack. Hundreds more charged Custer from his backside "like a hurricane, . . . like bees swarming out of a hive."[3] One First Nations eyewitness recalled, "The smoke of the shooting and the dust of the horses shut out the hill. And the soldiers fired many shots, but the Sioux shot straight. . . . When we came to the hill there were no soldiers living, and Long Hair [Custer] lay dead among the rest. . . . The blood of the people was hot and their hearts bad, and they took no prisoners that day."[4]

This "glorious hour" carried Sitting Bull to the crest of his power. But the victory was short-lived. The demise of Custer became the beginning of the end for the Sioux.

Hardin, Montana, July 4, 1998, twilight

Today I explore the Custer Battlefield, tossed by confused feelings. Nostalgia. Anger. Sadness. Revulsion. Admiration.

In the late afternoon, I drive on to my campground. I sit by the KOA pool and try to unwind, but my thoughts spin. Why did all this happen? And why is it happening again in Kosovo, Rwanda, Israel—nearly all over the world?

Are we doomed, O Lord? "Forgive us our trespasses." And "may thy will be done on earth, as it is in heaven."

Before falling asleep I hear popping sounds. Two miles south, fireworks rise over Hardin, Montana—and over thousands of American towns. But I do not feel like celebrating the Fourth of July. I will fall asleep wishing some loved ones were near.

Homesick.

Tonight I am longing for a homeland.

But where is my home?

Backlash

Newspapers described the defeat of Custer as "a massacre by the savages." This triggered fear and rage among whites. Sitting Bull could not be found, so the U.S. military declared war on all First Nations people in the West—even those on the reservation who had been nowhere near the Little Big Horn.

Homeland-longings gone terribly awry.

In the spring of 1877, Sitting Bull and his band of Hunkpapa Sioux fled north into Canada, which he called "the Land of the Grandmother" after Queen Victoria. Sitting Bull begged the queen to grant him a small reservation where his people could continue the old Sioux way of life.

The Royal Northwest Mounted Police, based at Wood Mountain under Superintendent James Morrow Walsh, feared Sitting Bull's arrival. How could the handful of police officers scattered through the Canadian plains forcibly eject four thousand Sioux who were fresh off the "Custer massacre"?[5]

Wisely, Walsh went to meet Sitting Bull, and the two carved out terms for a peaceful stay. However, by 1881 Sitting Bull had worn out his Canadian welcome. For one thing, the Sioux were expensive guests; with wild game too scarce to feed several thousand Hunkpapa mouths, the Canadian government and some private businessmen felt constrained to help—a costly proposition, to say the least. For another, Sitting Bull had become something of a political pariah. The U.S. government perceived its Canadian neighbor to be harboring a fugitive from American justice, and relations between Ottawa and Washington were strained as a result.

Then Mother Nature helped out the government and the RNMP. Prairie fires wiped out the grass, and a bitter winter killed most of the Hunkpapa ponies. The Sioux began drifting back across the border, until only a small, ragged band of sick and elderly remained in Canada with Sitting Bull.

Finally on July 19, 1881, Sitting Bull and his pitiful remnant left Willow Bunch, Saskatchewan, crossed the border to Montana, and reluctantly surrendered to the U.S. authorities at Fort Buford. According to reports, "He was wearing a tattered calico shirt, a pair of shabby leggings, and a dirty blanket. He looked old and beaten when he surrendered his rifle."[6]

Sitting Bull and the Sioux people were completely without a homeland.

Somehow Sitting Bull drew the attention of Buffalo Bill Cody; and for a short time, the chief toured with Cody's Wild West Show, becoming an international celebrity. After that brief hour in the sun, however, he settled down to a benign reservation farming life for which he was ill-suited.

Dance of Death

Meanwhile a strange religious man named Kicking Bear, a Miniconjou Lakota, was spreading the news that "the Messiah" had appeared among the First Nations. Kicking Bear convinced thousands of his people to wear "ghost shirts" that would keep the white man's bullets from hurting them and to dance a "ghost dance" that would make all the whites go away, bring the dead First Nations people back to life, and return the buffalo herds.

The Ghost Dancer phenomenon spread like wildfire across the plains, especially among a Miniconjou band led by an old chief named Big Foot. The government mistook it for an uprising. Some officials blamed Sitting Bull—although he had no part in the movement—and a warrant was issued for his arrest.

In his classic book, *Bury My Heart at Wounded Knee,* Dee Brown describes what happened next:

Just before daybreak, December 15, 1890, forty-three Indian police, many of whom had once been his fellow warriors, surrounded Sitting Bull's log cabin. They found him asleep on the floor and unceremoniously forced him half-naked from his bed out in front of the whole village.

Someone fired a shot, a melee broke out, and Sitting Bull was murdered.[7]

And so ended one story of a homeland lost.

For, whether in mid-sea or 'mong the breakers of the
farther shore, a wreck at last must mark the end of
each and all. And every life, no matter if its every
hour is rich with love and every moment jeweled
with a joy, will, at its close, become a tragedy
as sad and deep and dark as can be woven from
the warp and woof of mystery and death.

—ROBERT G. INGERSOLL

CHAPTER SEVEN

DRIVEN FROM HOME

Driven by fear of a Ghost Dancer uprising, the military chased down Chief Big Foot and his people, leading to a black day of horror at Wounded Knee Creek, South Dakota.

In the summer of 1998, I wandered over the site of the Wounded Knee Massacre. My journal reflects the day's turbulent feelings:

Spearfish, South Dakota, July 2, 1998

> *I leave Oglala, South Dakota, on Pine Ridge Reservation and pick my way toward Wounded Knee, feeling a strange mixture of foreboding and excitement. As I drive up to the site of the massacre, a cemetery and monument on top of the hill seem strangely familiar. Three days ago in Colorado Springs, my daughter Michele and I watched* Thunderheart, *a movie set on Pine Ridge Reservation. The movie repeatedly returned to the Wounded Knee Monument. Now here stands the monument in "real time" on the hill where the four Hotchkiss guns stood just after Christmas in 1890, the*

day they ripped the Miniconjou to fragments.

I pull off the road under the shade of a cottonwood tree. I dig out my book and my folding chair, climb the hill, and sit in the cemetery over which the monument stands watch. I open Dee Brown's Bury My Heart at Wounded Knee *and reread his account of the slaughter.*

The Surrender of Big Foot

It went something like this: When Big Foot learned of Sitting Bull's death, he knew that he and his people, the Miniconjou, were in danger too. Although he was ill with pneumonia and coughing blood, Big Foot moved his people through the brutal winter weather toward Pine Ridge, South Dakota, where he hoped powerful and peaceful Chief Red Cloud could protect him.

On the trail the group fatefully stumbled upon the very soldiers, led by Major Samuel Whitside, who were under orders to arrest Big Foot. Big Foot ran up a truce sign and rose from his blankets to greet Whitside. According to Dee Brown, "Big Foot's blankets were stained with blood from his lungs. . . . He talked in a hoarse whisper, . . . and red drops fell from his nose and froze in the bitter cold."[1]

Whitside explained that he had orders to take Big Foot's people to Wounded Knee Creek to link up with other cavalry. Big Foot was mercifully loaded into a heated ambulance wagon and, once at Wounded Knee camp, moved to a heated tent. Whitside carefully counted the First Nations people: 120 men,

230 women and children. To make sure no one escaped, Whitside stationed two Hotchkiss guns on the hill overlooking the camp—"positioned," as Brown explains, "to rake the length of the Indian lodges."[2]

In the night the seventh regiment—formerly Custer's regiment—arrived under the command of Colonel James Forsythe. This further terrified the helpless captives, who were mostly families of warriors who had fought Custer and now feared the army's revenge. Forsythe had orders to disarm the First Nations people but decided that he had better wait till morning. (Scott Vaughn, one of the Flying W Wranglers of Colorado Springs, once showed me documents naming his great-grandfather, John Shangreua, as the person who persuaded Forsythe not to disarm the First Nations warriors that night, because he knew the state of mind they were in).[3]

Forsythe placed two more Hotchkiss guns on the knoll near the two that were already there. Then he and his men opened a cask of whiskey and settled down to "celebrate the capture of Big Foot."[4]

The next morning after breakfast, the disarmament began. White Lance, a Wounded Knee survivor, recalled later, "So all of us gave the guns, and they were stacked up in the center."[5]

Bury My Heart

Exactly what happened next is uncertain, but some historians say that someone tried to pull a new Winchester from the hands of a young deaf man named Black Coyote. The Winchester discharged loudly, apparently hitting no one, but triggering an absolute disaster. Soldiers began shooting. First Nations men grabbed weapons from the pile and shot back. Soldiers and warriors fell into hand-to-hand combat. Brown writes, "Then the big Hotchkiss guns on the hill cut loose, firing almost a shell a second, raking the Indian camp, shredding the tepees with flying shrapnel, killing men, women, and children."[6]

When the gunfire finally subsided, 153 First Nations people, including Chief Big Foot himself, were dead, and scores more were seriously wounded. Women and children fled, crawling through the bushes, only to be chased down and slaughtered. The final death toll was nearly three hundred Miniconjou men, women, and children, plus several soldiers.

The surviving First Nations people were loaded into wagons and jostled some thirty miles through the bitter cold to Pine Ridge, where they were taken to shelter in an Episcopal mission. The date was December 29, 1890—just a few days after Christmas. A banner hung above the pulpit:

PEACE ON EARTH, GOOD WILL TO MEN[7]

Wounded Knee, South Dakota, July 2, 1998

I close the book, and my gut churns. My eyes flood.

I walk into the cemetery, where the inscription on the gray stone pillar declares, "This monument erected by the surviving relatives of Oglala and Cheyenne River Sioux Indian peoples, and in memory of the Chief Big Foot Massacre, December 29, 1890. . . . Many innocent women and children who knew no wrong died here."

I stand before the monument and speak each name out loud, feeling as if, somehow, this keeps their memories alive: "Chief Big Foot, Mr. High Hawk . . ." Name after name: "Mr. Shady Bear, Lost Wolf, Ghost Horse . . ." To the last name: "Kills Seneca."

Nearby tourists glance furtively, as if they think me drunk or imbalanced. And I don't care. I gather my things and stumble down the hill. I start the engine, pull out onto the blacktop, and drive northwest across the Pine Ridge Reservation.

Spearfish, South Dakota, July 2, 1998

This evening I sit by the KOA pool under the slanting rays of the late afternoon sun, cold drink in hand, overwhelmed by melancholy. The last desperate vestige of dignity for the Sioux ended, as T. S. Eliot might have observed, "with a whimper."

Under the slogan of "manifest destiny," immigrants shot down the native people, starved them out, and took their homeland. Before then, nearly 136 million First Nations peoples freely roamed 100 percent of the continent and called it home. Today only thirty-two million are left, living on less than 3 percent of the land. As Kevin Costner grippingly laments in the epilogue to the grand movie Dances with Wolves, "The great horse culture of the plains was gone, and the American frontier was about to pass into history."

A homeland lost!

Lord, help me never to forget this day.

Finally, after I eat a few bites of Vienna sausage and cheese, I crawl into my sleeping bag and dream of First Nations children crying for their parents. Crying for home.

Whose Home Is It?

And so the inexorable force of home-longing rolls on. Europeans searching for a homeland drive Sitting Bull from his. He in turn longs for land in Canada—land that was home to the Cree and the Blackfoot before him. Later my grandfather and my father homestead that same land, and I for a time claim it as my home. New strangers claim it now. Still others will in the future.

No one ever has or ever will hold this piece of land permanently. Not the First Nations people. Not my father. Certainly not me.

Whose home is it really?

Where is home?

Oh, where is home?

PART THREE

I WANT TO GO HOME

I wanna go home, I wanna go home.
Oh how I wanna go home.

—OLD AMERICAN FOLK SONG

My footsteps carry me away,
But in my mind I'm always going home.

—JOE DIFFIE

To be homeless the way people
like you and me are apt to be homeless
is to have homes all over the place but not
to be really at home in any of them.

—FREDRICK BUECHNER

I have become an alien in a foreign land.

—MOSES

CHAPTER EIGHT

ALIEN IN ALL PLACES

Sometimes it seems this wanderlust—this sense of chronic displacement—may be congenital and hereditary. That's what my son Chris seemed to be telling me the other day. I've heard him say something like this before, but never quite so poignantly.

Chris is a photojournalist. Born in Canada, raised in Texas, he carries both Canadian and American passports. After college he left Texas to work for a while for a newspaper in Colorado. Later, based in New York, he trotted the globe doing assignments for numerous magazines. Now he lives in Paris, far from his roots, both geographically and culturally. And for years his camera and his heart have captured various theaters of war and human suffering up close: Haiti, Sarajevo, Kosovo, Afghanistan, Israel, Iraq. Chris is often in several countries during any particular month and never very long in any one place, not even his Paris apartment.

During a recent time together, I felt a rush of profound connection with Chris when he looked at me in a most haunting way and said, "Dad, I feel homeless." I knew exactly what he meant—even though, I have to say, my son seems to have taken the congenital Anderson wanderlust to extremes.

Wandering Feet

When I left high school at age eighteen, my wandering feet took me away from the world of my childhood to college in the southern United States, far, far from home. Much happened during the five years that followed my initial immersion into new cultural perspectives and new worlds of academic thought. Marriage to Carolyn. Graduate studies. University-level doubts. Our first child. A budding ministry. A whole new circle of friends. The list could continue for pages. In the process I took on the "you-all-ism" of the American South. Those first few years in the South changed me so significantly—and lastingly—that I was no longer sure where home was.

By the time I moved back to Canada, my fatherland no longer felt fully like home. It didn't help that I settled in a part of Canada that was new to me—British Columbia—some nine hundred miles west of my prairie roots, into a Rocky Mountain culture that was very different from life on the plains. So although I was (and am still) a Canadian citizen, I felt somewhat like an alien in my own country. At the same time, since I wasn't (and am not) an American citizen, the southern United States—the place I'd just left—didn't seem like home either.

Ever since I have felt like a chronic wanderer. Root-confused!

This root confusion invaded my graduate work. The title of my master's thesis was "American Ministers in Canadian Situations: A Study in Cross-Cultural Communication." The stated purpose was to help American ministers understand the huge subterranean differences in world-view between the two North American cultures that look so much alike on the surface. In retrospect, I know the project was more an elaborate attempt to sort out who I really am.

Henri Nouwen described the sense of rootlessness and alienation he felt when he left his family in Holland and moved to the United States, then to South America, then to Canada. A misfit as a priest within his own secularized Dutch family, he searched constantly for a true home. Nouwen said he was never able to resolve the restlessness but learned to live with it "as some people must learn to manage a chronic physical pain: 'you do not run away from it but feel it through and stand up in it and look it right in the face.' "[1]

Pulling Up Stakes

I began to "feel through" my own restlessness those first several years of marriage, when Carolyn and I lived in a number of rented homes: campus apartments; a tiny cottage; a skid shack in Salmon Arm, British Columbia, with two stingy bedrooms and one tiny bath.

Eventually, in Kelowna, B.C., we scraped together enough money for a down payment on a house. Our "first home," the real-estate agents called it. I guess I thought home ownership would clarify my identity and resolve the restlessness. But even though our family lived in that house for a number of years, it wasn't really our home. We merely had our names on a piece of paper that said we could stay there as long as we sent the bank a little money every month. We didn't actually *own* it. The people who were in the house before us had lived there under similar arrangements. By now several subsequent "owners" have sojourned in the place.

Paying a mortgage dispelled none of my alien-wandering feelings. And eleven years after arriving in beautiful British Columbia, I wandered again. This time we moved to—of all places—Abilene, Texas. Talk about feeling displaced! Back in Kelowna, spectacular natural beauty surrounded us on every side. From our living room window we could see the snow-crowned tip of Big White Ski Hill. Less than a mile behind our house, the clear waters of Okanagan Lake lazily caressed miles of sandy beach. But Abilene, Texas?

Don't misunderstand me. The people in Abilene are wonderful. But one visitor from Georgia, upon first sight of the West Texas landscape, wondered aloud if there had been a nuclear blast. For a family acclimated to the Canadian Rockies, West Texas was *certainly* not home.

Yet again, out of longing to put down roots, we purchased five acres outside of Abilene and built a house. Of course, we called that place our home. We lived there almost twenty years.

Reared our children there. Our church became as much family to us as any people on the face of the earth.

Still Homeless

But Abilene is not home. Our children no longer live there, nor do we. We left that house twelve years ago, and it has changed hands twice since then. Today, strangers live there and pay the bank for the privilege. (Actually, the bank has changed hands several times too.)

We moved again—this time to Dallas. To an empty nest. To a church that did not know our children. To yet another cultural setting. And to a church parsonage that didn't belong to us. Our names weren't even on the papers at the bank. With my parents deceased, our children scattered, and familiar scenes gone, at times I felt an overwhelming longing to go home. But I had no idea where to go.

I was fifty-five and homeless.

Furthermore, I had no idea who I was. I still wonder. My paternal roots are Swedish. Maternal, German. I hold Canadian citizenship but have now lived in Texas for more than thirty-two years. I am still not an American—and certainly not a bona fide Texan (although we love our current house in the pictur-esque and historic hill country outside San Antonio). Canada is no longer my home, but neither is the United States. I don't feel at home in either place.

Am I a Swede? A German? A Canadian? An American? A

country boy? A city boy? Who am I, and where do I belong? I long for a homeland, but I have lost the internal map to get me there. Don't guess I will ever find it. Sometimes it seems that I am destined, like my father, my grandfather, and his father before him, to wander the earth till Jesus comes, always longing for a homeland but never feeling at home no matter where I am. The first time I read these lines from Bojer's *The Emigrants,* I wept:

> *If you came back*
> *You wanted to leave again.*
> *If you went away*
> *You longed to come back.*
> *Wherever you were*
> *You could hear the call of the homeland,*
> *Like the note of the herdsman's horn*
> *Far away in the hills.*
> *You had one home out there,*
> *And one home over here,*
> *And yet you were an alien*
> *In both places.*
> *Your true abiding place*
> *Was the vision of something very far off.*
> *And your soul was like the waves,*
> *Always restless,*
> *Forever in motion.*[2]

I understand, Mr. Bojer. Indeed I do.

PART FOUR

IN ALL THE WRONG PLACES

We have been lost ever since we left Eden,
wandering the world, looking for home,
and getting mighty dirty in the process.

—AUTHOR UNKNOWN

And I will bring you to the land
I swore with uplifted hand to give
to Abraham, to Isaac and to Jacob.
I will give it to you as a possession.
I am the LORD.

—EXODUS 6:8

Breathes there the man with soul so dead,

Who never to himself hath said,

"This is my own, my native land!"

Whose heart hath ne'er within him burn'd,

As home his footsteps he hath turn'd,

From wandering on a foreign strand?

—SIR WALTER SCOTT

CHAPTER NINE

THE OLD HOMEPLACE

Heinrich Uthoff tried to ride a train back to a place in the heart. He was another of those fascinating, soul-mate "searchers" I met on the VIA train during my sentimental journey across Canada. Heinrich left his heart prints on my journal:

Aboard the VIA train, Sioux Lookout, Ontario, August 28, 1994

> *Heinrich Uthoff tells me that when he was a young paratrooper during World War II, the German Luftwaffe dropped him into Holland, where he was immediately captured by Allied soldiers and shipped to a POW camp in Canada. Heinrich spent part of his five POW years in Lethbridge, Alberta. Canada was experiencing a wartime farm-labor shortage, so prisoners like Heinrich were put to work in the fields.*
>
> *"In 1940, while in POW camp in Lethbridge," Heinrich recounts, "I married my back-home German sweetheart—by proxy, while she was in Germany and I in Canada." Now at over eighty years of age, the Uthoffs have come over from Germany*

and are riding this train to Lethbridge to celebrate their fiftieth anniversary. "My bride wants to see—for the first time—the place where I married her!" Heinrich glows.

Dusseldorf friends launched the Uthoffs on this journey. Lethbridge friends will welcome them. In fact, Lethbridge has actually funded the trip and is planning a huge celebration. Frau Uthoff tells me, "Though I have never been there, I feel as if Lethbridge is in some way partly my home."

Oh yes, Heinrich and Frau Uthoff, we all want to get back to someplace. And we sometimes try to "go home again" in the strangest of ways.

Longing for place is as at least as old as the Psalms. Listen to the soul of this homesick Hebrew poet, writing from exile: "By the rivers of Babylon we sat and wept when we remembered Zion. . . . How can we sing the songs of the LORD while in a foreign land? . . . May my tongue cling to the roof of my mouth if I do not remember you, if I do not consider Jerusalem my highest joy" (Psalm 137:1-6).

Road to Disappointment

There are special places on this earth where some of us have felt peace. Places where important memories were born. Places that once felt like home way back in some long ago time. Most of us eventually leave them. We take different roads away from the old homeplace. From time to time we long to go back. But when and if we ever do get back, we only discover, to our sad disappointment, that Thomas Wolfe was right: You can't go home again.

Nevertheless, we keep trying.

Some searchers reach their homeland. Some don't. Many ancient Israelites finally entered the Promised Land. Many did not.

Abraham saw the land. Even set foot on it. But camping there was as close as he came to living on that homeland. He was always moving. Searching. Longing for something that even that God-promised piece of real estate could not give him.

Arriving at last in Canaan did not really get his descendants where they longed to be either. Even the Promised Land wasn't home in the deepest sense. What is more, they could not seem to hold on to it permanently. Twice in Scripture God expelled them from the land. Then brought them back in again. Indeed, the Jews have wandered in and out of that land for millennia. In and out. Back and forth. Until they were eventually scattered like dust across the face of the earth.

In 1945 the Hebrew people began yet another attempt to reclaim their land. But to date they have recovered merely a scrap of what they once called home. And even that scrap is held very precariously and at the price of ongoing bloodshed, because the Palestinians—who are also descendants of Abraham—claim the promise too. Some Palestinians even appeal to the New Testament, where Galatians chapter 4 seems to indicate that the "Jerusalem which now is" (v. 25 NKJV) belongs to the children of the slave woman, Hagar—that is, the Arabs.

No one can promise either Jews or Palestinians that their home-longings will be resolved any time soon. More poignant still: Even if the "correct" descendants of Abraham get back all the real estate they consider their promised land, it will not make them feel at home in the fullest sense.

Thousands of immigrants to the United States ended up on land of their own. Their first residences may have been tents or dugouts on the open prairies or log cabins among timber-laden hills—but at least they were their own. Yet I suspect that after longing for and finally finding their very own "forty acres and mule," most still died feeling somewhat disappointed, somewhat less than fully home.

Deep down, I think most of us do.

In my own small way, I share the homeland-longing of both Israelites and immigrants. Lord knows I have more than once returned to the homeplace of my childhood, trying to "get back home" by walking once again on the land my Grandpa Eric homesteaded. Land where I was born and lived until my early teens, then left, never to live there again. But as the old Stamps-Baxter spiritual says it, "I can't feel at home in this world any more"—not even back on the old homeplace.

A Shattered Dream

Memories of my first attempt to take my children back home still bring a lump to my throat. I was all ajitter with anticipation that day, heading south from McCord, Saskatchewan, down the twelve-mile road toward my childhood home, seventeen rangeland miles from Montana. I babbled old family legends the whole way, hoping my children would catch the spirit of the old homeplace. I wanted them to experience with me the home-feelings from long ago. But far before we reached the homestead, things looked wrong. Old dirt roads had disappeared beneath gravel and blacktop. Most familiar landmarks had vanished. *Where had these new farmhouses come from?* When I was a child, we hailed everyone along this road by name. Now strange faces stared curiously back through pickup windshields.

Even the hills seemed smaller.

In spite of these changes, when I drove through the gate onto our land, I still felt intoxicated with a mixture of nostalgia and excitement. I couldn't wait to show my kids the panoramic view from atop the big hill, where the ancient smoke-signal hearth still keeps watch. To walk them through the circles of stones where tepees once stood. To climb with them up to the big spring that once watered our herd, and to the First Nations graves that look down from a low hill across the old wheat field and hay slew on the west side.

I wanted my children to connect with simple objects from my childhood. The ruins of the 1929 Pontiac in which I learned to drive, eyes peeking over the dash, feet stretching for the pedals. The old sleigh still resting on a knoll: My sisters and I ran along behind it to warm our toes. The rusty remains of Dad's old grain binder. Object after object, memory after nostalgic memory.

Not a Place

We drove down through the gully, past the old well, and up toward the yard where my small-boy bare feet used to run. But I was not prepared for what hit me when we pulled up in front of the old house. Weeds and grass, waist high, had taken over what had once been Mother's well-kept yard lined with shrubs and flowers. The outbuildings had all crumbled into the past. But the old house still stood—alone—her features weathered by time and vacancy, yet her personality and character still intact. However, she looked so very forlorn. Remnants of the brick chimney leaned off-angle, about to tumble through a gap where the winds of fifty winters had wiggled shingles loose. Pigeons fluttered out of these holes in the roof. Partly broken windows stared blankly, like the eyes of a lunatic gone mad with loneliness.

For long moments I could only stand and stare back. Time seemed to fall away. I felt my bare feet running though the grass again. Heard my sisters laughing as young girls. Smelled Mom's cooking. Heard Dad's tenor song. An ache several levels deeper than physical pressed around my heart. I reeled under the storm of nostalgia.

Then suddenly, like awakening from a dream, yesterday fell away.

CHAPTER NINE: THE OLD HOMEPLACE

My children tugged at my coat. "Daddy, why are you crying?"

How could I explain to them that here in the very center of my childhood place, I felt anything but at home? Never had the words of Thomas Wolfe seemed more poignantly, personally true: No, I couldn't go home again. Home would never *be* again. Only in memory. Nothing more. Even if the buildings had not decayed, it still would have been impossible to get home by coming to this place. The "home-ness" of the old homeplace had been erased forever. My soul felt as empty as that old house.

Mom and Dad have long since gone to heaven. They hadn't been to the homeplace for at least a decade before they died. One of my sisters is buried a thousand miles away; the three living sisters, scattered across the earth. Even old neighbors have died or left. Only the land remains the same—yet even it seems different: Once tilled and fenced for fields, it is now turned back to rangeland at the hands of strangers.

That day I began to comprehend on profoundly unsettling levels that *home is not a place*. The old homeplace is not home. In fact, no *place* is. Not for me. And, I think, not for anyone.

Moses, did you once feel that Egypt was really your home? What's that? Never completely so? Deep down inside, Moses, under all the regal trappings, did your child-heart sense that you didn't really belong in that palace? Somehow you knew that you were not a true son of Egyptian soil. Did that slumbering awareness burst wide-awake that day you fled as a fugitive from your forty-year childhood homeplace? That first night beside the desert refugee trail when you pillowed your head on the sand—what dark, sad, homeless soliloquy flooded your mind?

In those following forty years, Moses, did you feel homesickness in Midian? You picked up work there and seemed firmly rooted on your father-in-law's land. But Jethro's land was no more your home, Moses, no more your land than Egypt had been in the past or the wilderness would be in the future. As with all your dwelling places, you only stopped a while in Jethro's pasture on your way to somewhere else. In all that time, you never owned an acre of ground for yourself, did you? You were a hired hand. Carrying a green card. Just passing through. When God called to you from the burning bush, you knew Midian would never be home again, didn't you?

And oh, Moses, how did you handle those final forty years? Wandering in the wilderness on lands that belonged to this people and that—people who didn't adopt you as a son nor hire you as a hand? You were more like a constant trespasser. A homeless street person. A man without a country!

"Of course," some would explain on your behalf, "Canaan was Moses' real homeland—the land of God's promise. And Moses knew that." Yet the truth is, you knew better. And in the end, Moses, you didn't go to Canaan either. Turned out, it wasn't your homeland after all.

Oh no, friend Moses, home is not a place. Never has been.

Not for me. And not for you. Not even if the place is real estate promised by God Almighty.

Granted, for those who can stay in one location for a while, a physical, geographical place may actually seem like home. No question, some people do stay on the land longer than others.

Mark Elford has.

When my father was a young Christian, his spiritual mentor was a neighbor, Russell Elford. Russell had been only seventeen years of age and his bride, Annie, just fifteen when they weathered their first winter in the West. He was a giant of a man, with a barrel chest, hands like hams, a voice like gentle thunder—and a passion for Jesus Christ. Among my early memories of church is listening to Brother Elford sing—every word of every hymn belted with gusto at the top of his voice, and all on one note.

Russell passed his land to his son George, and George to his sons Mark and Glenn. Mark is still there. He loves his ancestral homeland and dreams that his grandsons will one day run the ranch, now many times its original land size.

Last June one of my sons, one of my sons-in-law, my two grandsons, and I rode horseback for two days across the south Saskatchewan hills with Mark Elford and others. Mark's love of the place is so contagious that my boys, too, fell in love with the way of life on this rangeland.

Recently, Rural Route Videos of Saskatchewan produced a piece called *The Canadian Rancher*, a documentary of the Elfords' ranching operation with Mark narrating. In the touching closing moments of the video, Mark looks into the camera and says, his voice catching a bit, "It would kill me to ever lose this place."[1]

While Mark Elford's love of the soil touches deep places in my heart, yet even deeper down I find my soul crying out.

You will be separated from that land, Mark. Sooner or later, one way or the other. So will your sons. My grandfather and father were separated from theirs in one way, your grandfather and then your father in another. I was separated from my home-place too! You can't hold this land forever. Besides, you and I both know, in our soul of souls:

Home is not a place.

When a man goes to visit his boyhood town,
he goes to visit his boyhood.

—MARK TWAIN

Let me go back to my own people.

—MOSES

CHAPTER TEN

THE FOLKS BACK HOME

While the Texas sunset spread across the western sky, Lance and Eddie sat on the back deck, talking of homesickness. Lance's words moved slowly, wistfully.

"I didn't expect it to be like that. Hadn't been back to Greene County, Ohio, since the year I graduated high school. Up that way on business last month, I got this strong hankerin' to go see the country place where I grew up. Felt as disappointed as a six-year-old when he finds out about Santa Claus. Just wasn't the same."

The evening grew still, the sun a red ball on the edge of the prairie. Neither man spoke for a long spell.

Then Lance continued wistfully, "I couldn't get back home. And I don't much like that feeling."

With a last pink hint, the sky remembered that the sun had just set, and locusts tuned up in the cedar bush before Eddie eventually responded.

"Of course goin' there wouldn't give you the feeling of home, Lance. Home isn't a *place*. It's the folks that live there."

Lance looked at Eddie, then back into the gathering dark. "Guess that's right," Lance conceded. Then, after a long moment, "And when those folks are gone, it sure ain't home no more."

Do I see you nodding your head, friend reader, maybe even blinking back a tear? Of course we know that: A place back down the years somewhere, a place that we call "home," only feels like home if "our people" still live there. The bard who gave us the nostalgic song "I'll Be Home for Christmas" intended to be with family for the holidays—regardless of whether they now lived in Los Angeles, California, or Little Bluff, Kansas. Indeed, over a lifespan, most families will live in a number of different places. Many houses. One home.

The feeling called "home" is obviously far more about relationships than about real estate. Far more about a *people* than a *place*. As Edgar A. Guest reminded us:

> It takes a heap o' livin' in a house t' make it home,
> A heap o' sun an' shadder, an' ye sometimes have t' roam
> Afore ye really 'preciate the things ye lef' behind,
> An' hunger fer 'em somehow—with 'em allus on yer mind.
>
> . . . .
>
> Home ain't a place that gold can buy or get up in a minute;
> Afore it's home there's got t' be a heap o' livin' in it.[1]

Visiting Our Folks

"Going home" is going to visit the home folks. We spare no trouble or expense getting together with loved ones on special occasions. (Even the writing of this book was gladly interrupted by a long-awaited family reunion.) "Happy Birthday" sounds best when the whole family sings it together. The more loved ones we have gathered around the Thanksgiving table, the more delicious the turkey and dressing. And on Christmas morning, we wait to open gifts until the whole family is gathered around the tree.

It seems obvious that family must be our home, our place to belong. Even people who have no family expend much of life's energy trying to make a family or find a family or at least create the illusion of a family.

So, like most folk, I've gone back to see family as often as possible. And, like most folk, I've called it "going home," even when it meant going to the strange house my parents occupied in Weyburn, Saskatchewan, their last thirty-five years. I never lived there. Didn't know the town. Or the neighbors. But I wasn't going home to see a place; I was going home to see my people. My parents. Sisters. Brothers-in-law. Nieces. Nephews. Cousins.

Across time, however, each visit seemed less and less like going home. Each year my parents knew less about my world, and I'd drifted further out of touch with theirs. Drifted even further from my extended family. We scattered. Now siblings see each other less and less frequently. Our life paths grow ever further apart. We have different circles of relationships. Different life issues and interests. I am losing track of nieces and nephews. Don't remember the names of all their children.

For decades now I have felt my family gradually crumbling into history.

Sharing Foundations

Family foundations felt their first major tremor during my mother's late stages of Parkinson's disease. At first she just wasn't herself. Somewhere in those dark, waning years, this woman who had always loved to cook all sorts of goodies for us, quit cooking. We joked, "Dad's not a bad cook, but not like Mom." We said those words, but we meant so much more. Dad doing the cooking merely symbolized the larger, more significant ways our foundations were shifting. The last several times I visited my mother, she only stared into space, showing no signs that she recognized me. I began to feel motherless.

Then came the day when Dad gathered his scattered children home around Mother's hospital bed. Amazingly, in those last few hours, she partly emerged from the fog. She recognized us. Showed interest in photographs. Laughed. Even talked a bit. As if she knew those were her last hours, Mom rallied her faculties for that final visit.

We siblings and Dad left the hospital shortly after noon to let Mom rest a bit, looking forward to another visit that evening. But shortly after we reached the house, a nurse called.

Mom was gone.

Even though she had not really been with us for several

years, still we felt a major earthquake. A huge chunk of home fell away. After that, going home was never quite the same.

My father's strength had always been nearly superhuman. When he was eighty years of age, people still took him to be in his early sixties. He was healthy, gregarious, and fun loving. But then somewhere in his eighties, under the strain of taking care of Mother, Dad became a withered old man, almost overnight.

My father was eighty-four and I was fifty-three when I finally became "Dr." Anderson. Dad's last hurrah for the world was to make the trip south to Texas for the commencement ceremonies. Shortly after, Dad returned home to Canada; and in a few months, we could see that he was dying. Cancer spread through his body and finally invaded his brain, leaving stroke-like symptoms.

Carolyn and I flew to Saskatchewan, intending to spend those final days with him. But he rallied in a week or so, and we headed back to Dallas—arriving only to receive a call from my sister saying that Dad had taken a turn for the worse. The doctors suggested that we reassemble the family. So Carolyn and I packed hastily, climbed into the car, and set out on a rainy Saturday night on the three-day drive from Dallas back to Weyburn, Saskatchewan.

This was two-and-a-half weeks before Christmas.

We spent the next weeks at my father's bedside in Moose Jaw Union Hospital. He wanted his children near. I am his only son; so although he couldn't always form words, his eyes followed my every move around the room. Day after day his condition remained unchanged but unpredictable.

Christmas was fast approaching, and we knew our children were expecting us in Colorado Springs for the holiday season. Carolyn and I felt torn, not wanting to leave my father, yet not wanting to disappoint our kids. Finally we decided to rush to Colorado for Christmas and then hurry back to Dad.

I sat down by my father's bedside and awkwardly attempted to explain our plans. Dad shook his head repeatedly and finally managed to get out the words "I—won't be—here."

"Of course you will, Dad," I assured him. But Dad turned his face away and would not look at me again as I kept repeating, "Only a few days . . ."

Oddly, the last words I said to my father I spoke to the back of his head. Although we loved each other enormously, Dad and I were turning away from each other. I was leaving him, and he was leaving me. I kissed him good-bye and left for Colorado.

Home was slipping away at a dark and frightening speed.

The dreaded call reached us in Colorado Springs on Christmas Eve.

Dad was gone.

This was certainly not the most joyful Christmas on record. I felt dead inside. And torn—in one moment, grateful that my children were around me in this time of grief. The next moment, guilt ridden that I had not been with Dad when his last hour came. And while I wanted our children and grandchildren to have a happy Christmas season, at the same time, I inflicted a lot of my convoluted grief on the family. I did and said foolish and angry things I would long regret.

A Storm of Passage

The day after Christmas, Carolyn and I pulled out of Colorado Springs for the two-day drive back to Saskatchewan for Dad's funeral. The first day we made good time in beautiful weather. The second morning we set out under fair skies. But shortly after midday, an ominous cloud bank formed on the horizon, and a north wind rose. The temperature began a free fall from about 55 degrees above to 15 degrees below in a matter of two or three hours. Long before we reached the Canadian border, we had traveled dozens of miles into a blinding snowstorm. Yet we drove on, because Dad's funeral was set for the next day.

Darkness gathered while we checked through the Canadian border. And with every passing mile, we became more and more aware that we were facing the mother of all blizzards. Snow grew thicker. The wind kept rising. The mercury kept falling. Visibility rapidly diminished. But we dismissed the idea of stopping, because home was only a hundred miles up the road.

Home?

So we drove on into the howling, frozen night. Our car radio kept telling us the blizzard was widespread, would grow worse, would likely last for two or three days. The Mounties were warning travelers to get off the highways, which made reaching our destination seem all the more urgent.

Soon the blinding glare of snow whirling past our headlights made visibility impossible. So with parking lights only, we crept along between those lines where the edge of the dark pavement met the vast whiteness. Periodic flurries wrapped us in total whiteout. At times I literally had to get out of the car to figure out where the road was. Each time the cold and wind quickly sucked my breath away and chilled me to the bone.

To make matters worse, we had left our warmest winter ski clothes behind in Colorado. The light coats we had with us could not begin to protect against such savage weather. According to the radio, temperatures had plunged past thirty below, with winds gusting over thirty-five miles an hour.

Then the unthinkable happened. At one curve I mistook the smoothly plowed snow on the shoulder for the roadway and drove straight into a ditch, high centering in bottomless whiteness. The car wouldn't budge. I crawled out to look for some kind of post, rock, or makeshift tool that might help us get unstuck, but I could endure the bitter wind only a few moments at a time.

Adding to our dismay, the radio listed our highway as now closed to traffic.

Winter experience in my growing-up years told me that our situation was desperate. Even with clothing equal to the weather and candles to warm the interior of the car—of which we had neither—survival would be difficult in that howling, once-in-a-decade blizzard. With our inadequate clothing and no candles, we would not likely outlast our half-tank of gasoline by more than a few hours. Carolyn and I actually began to think these were our last hours on earth, both silently trying to shape the way we would say good-bye to each other.

Road Angels

Then the first angel arrived. Out of the lethal white fury, a large grocery truck appeared. With chained wheels and headlights up high, the driver could see over the ground-blow well enough to follow the road. At risk to himself, the driver hooked a cable to our car and snaked us back onto the pavement.

Rescued.

We had no choice but to continue driving toward our destination, which we estimated was only about fifty miles ahead. But soon we discovered an additional handicap. Ice had gathered on our accelerator, leaving only two speeds: wide open and off. We had to crank up the car, yank it into gear, and let it gather speed until we reached forty or fifty miles an hour. Then we'd have to shut off the engine and coast to a near stop.

Repeating the process again and again, we limped along for some miles, until through the gloom we spotted a halo of light that turned out to be a lamppost at the cross streets of a little village. We could see no buildings—just the vast, whirling whiteness surrounding that pool of light. We pulled up under the lamppost, and once more I crawled out into the elements, hoping to free up the accelerator. But the cold literally took my breath away. I could stand it just long enough to learn that the hood was securely frozen shut.

What to do?

Enter angel number two.

A car emerged from the murk and pulled up beside us. A window slid open, and a young male voice spoke from the dark interior. "You'd better get off this road," he said pleasantly, pointing into the night. "A few yards that way, we have a heated implement shed. Run your car in there with our vehicles to thaw it out. Then jump in here with me, and I'll take you to the house. My mother has a hot supper on the stove. And a warm bed upstairs is just waiting for someone like you."

Rarely have we heard more welcome words. That night Carolyn and I slept "in the arms of angels," in a cozy upstairs bedroom of this strong Catholic family. As we were to learn around the dinner table, my brother-in-law had taught school in that community in past years. Some of his students had been this family's children! Carolyn and I fell asleep snug and safe in a warm bed, listening to the song of the prairie blizzard around the eaves, thankful to God and to these kind and hospitable people.

Next morning, the day of my father's funeral, the temperature still hovered at thirty-five below, with wind gusts up to thirty-five miles an hour. But the skies had cleared somewhat, the highway was freshly plowed, and our little Honda was now functioning perfectly.

We thanked our "angels" profusely and drove on, arriving in just enough time to dress for the funeral.

Demise of an Illusion

Although I fondly remember many happy family gatherings in my parents' house in Weyburn, the town had always seemed a bleak and depressing place to me. Even if this had not been the occasion of my father's death, Weyburn would have felt dismal. Now adding my soul-numbing grief and the killing blizzard to the mix, the town felt morose beyond expression. Even the funeral gathering was small. Folks dared not brave the weather.

Just one van followed the hearse to the cemetery, carrying only the pallbearers and our immediate family. The winds ripped across the gray tombstones with such cruelty that most of the family didn't leave the van. The pallbearers hurriedly settled Dad's casket onto the lowering device and scuttled back to the car for cover. The funeral director and I lingered a few more minutes. I wanted to say a final, personal good-bye to my father.

When the funeral director tripped the switch to lower the casket into the icy grave, the lowering device would not budge. It had frozen solid. As he fumbled with the mechanism, a waxen frostbite began claiming his face.

"You can come back and finish this when the weather breaks," I urged. "Dad is all right. He always loved a good blizzard anyway." We sprinted to the warmth of the hearse, leaving the casket on top of the ground in the vicious cold. For months afterward, I frequently dreamed that I saw my father lying out in a blizzard, dressed in a suit with no overcoat—but with a smile on his face.

Two days after the funeral, still under gray skies, surrounded by brutal cold, Carolyn and I said good-bye to family and friends and headed southward, driving wordlessly through the gloom. Not far out of town, I turned to Carolyn and broke the silence.

"I don't think I ever want to come back here again."

I felt as disconnected from "home-ness," from any sense of belonging, as I have ever felt in my life. In the words of the old spiritual, the "circle" definitely felt "broken." Of course, Carolyn was still with me, but in those hours I reluctantly began to face the fact that even she and I would not be with each other forever.

Oh yes, when the fields are green, I will go back to see my parents' graves and the land they once called theirs. I will take my children too, if I can. And tell them stories of their roots. But will I call it home?

Obviously I am not alone in this experience. A similar, sad separation drama has been replayed in every family among humankind—since long before the days of Moses' soul-crushing loss, when he was forced to flee the people who had been his family for forty years.

Moses, my friend, seems your meanderings were marked with final farewells. No doubt in your childhood you felt like an

Egyptian. You lived in the Pharaoh's family. Surely those familial relationships bonded you to King Pharaoh as his son and a prince of Egypt.

Ah, but you were no Egyptian. You were a Hebrew. When did you first feel this? In the end, of course, Moses, you chose to side with the people of your blood, and you walked away from the princely position you had known from birth. Still, surely you left feeling homeless. In those first few months after you were forced out of your house and fled your royal family, how many nights did you cry yourself to sleep? We still hear you weeping out your homesickness: "I have become an alien in a foreign land" (Exodus 2:22).

Oh yes, Moses, you forever left fond relationships behind, because you knew that Pharaoh's family was not your people.

And it didn't stop there, did it, friend Moses? You spent a second forty years gathering another family, running down roots as Jethro's son-in-law, only to face the fact that the Midianites were not your people either. You revisited the same searing grief of separation when the Mighty One moved you away once more from folks that had come to feel like family. Away from home again.

Moses, you were—you are—a Hebrew. Your people were the Israelites. That is why you "chose to be mistreated along with the people of God" (Hebrews 11:25) rather than cling to Pharaoh's privilege or Jethro's peace. God called you out of a secure and quiet life as a Midianite sheep rancher to endure the hardship and danger of delivering your people through the wilderness into the Promised Land.

But then separation struck once more. In the end the people of Israel left you behind and went into the homeland without you, Moses. Without you! Again you were painfully parted from the people to whom your soul had been knit. That final day you walked out of the camp alone—with no people. You, too, friend Moses, long before me, found out:

Home is not a people.

Partings

Across the centuries, before Moses and since, people have been parting from their people. Measure, if you can, the grief in the hearts of the Sioux and the Apache and the Cherokee, driven brokenhearted from familiar places and faces to strange new terrain, as whole bands, whole villages, saw the bowl of their culture broken, the survivors left homeless and alone. Or the heartache of European emigrants pushed away from home and family by circumstances. Asian immigrants too. Africans pulled away by slavers. Middle Easterners. Latin Americans. They looked backward for the last time on familiar and precious faces, then turned and walked away—landless, homeless, alone. Most of these displaced persons never saw their loved ones again—even missed family funerals, sometimes receiving the sad news months later.

That cold day as we drove away from Dad's funeral, I personally discovered what humankind has been experiencing for ages. Oh yes, years earlier I had begun to learn that home is not a *place*. Places change. They go away. Or we do. I knew that. So I had come to hope that home was a *people—my people*. But how wrong I was on that score too! Home may appear for a time to be our people, but sooner or later, one way or another, we all leave each other.

Home is not a people. People won't stay with us.

Even if they did, no human relationship is ultimately fulfilling. Even the tightest and most ideal of friendships—or closest of families, or most intimate of marriages—leaves us partly lonely. Henri Nouwen explored the depths of this loneliness:

> We desire to break out of our isolation and loneliness and enter into a relationship that offers us a sense of home, an experience of belonging, a feeling of safety, and a sense of being well connected. But . . . when we are lonely and look for someone to take our loneliness away, we are quickly disillusioned. The *other*, who for a while may have offered us an experience of wholeness and inner peace, soon proves incapable of giving us lasting happiness, and instead of taking away our expectation that another human being will fulfill our deepest desires, the pain grows even greater when we are confronted with the limitations of human relationships.[2]

Of course I have often gone back to Weyburn (a rather pleasant town actually). Back again, when the grass has been green, to sit for a while at my parents' graves. And I have treasured those hours. But going there has not gotten me back home.

Home is not a people. No, not a place. And not a people. Never has been.

No human being can fill the longing for intimacy that only God can fill. In fact, while we are in this life, even our relationship with God isn't totally and ultimately fulfilling, because flesh veils him from us. Mortality limits our capacity for intimacy with him. We do not see him as he is; thus we cannot love him as we ought. Not yet. A line from the old '70s song by the 2nd Chapter of Acts underscores this limitation:

> *I'm not sayin' you don't give me joy,*
> *I just need more of you*
>
> . . . .
>
> *How I long to be there by your side,*
> *In your love*
> *In your hands.*
> *So take me home.*[3]

Ah yes. In this world we are all destined to a certain degree of loneliness and homesickness.

In *this* world.

Life is a narrow vale between the cold and barren peaks of two eternities. We strive in vain to look beyond the heights. We cry aloud—and the only answer is the echo of our wailing cry. From the voiceless lips of the unreplying dead there comes no word; but in the night of Death Hope sees a star and listening Love can hear the rustle of a wing.

—ROBERT G. INGERSOLL

For all can see that wise men die; the foolish and the
senseless alike perish and leave their wealth to others.
Their tombs will remain their houses forever,
their dwellings for endless generations, though they
had named lands after themselves.

—PSALM 49:10-11

CHAPTER ELEVEN

MY PLACE IN THE SUN

Cathy Meeks, protestor in the 1960s, felt a deep loss of identity. She felt torn between her religions roots, on the one hand, which she feared reinforced injustice, and a spirit of rebellion, on the other hand, which didn't square with her Christian upbringing. "She asked herself where she belonged," Jack Hayford observes in his book *The Heart of Praise*, "a question that raised deeper questions of who she was, down deep, and whether anyone really cared."[1]

This loss of connectedness led her to write her own book under the haunting title, *I Want Someone to Know My Name*. Hayford comments further: "We all need the reassurance that we aren't 'lost in space,' drifting among the stars, alone and unknown in the cosmos."[2]

Cathy, your questions probe my soul too. Your title captures my longing to make a difference and not be forgotten. But who does really care? Over time, even our families will forget us. So who really cares?

How much does one human being matter anyway? One tiny person? One mere speck of dust among five billion other specks of dust huddled on this planet? A planet which itself is only one tiny speck of dust in an immeasurably huge cloud of dust amid hundreds of millions of other clouds of dust—some particles of which are so large they would not fit between earth and sun—separated from one another by millions of light-years? What does a solitary human being amount to in this unfathomable vastness?

Questions like these surely spun through the mind of the psalmist who wrote, "When I consider your heavens, the work of your fingers, the moon and the stars, which you have set in place, what is man that you are mindful of him?" (Psalm 8:3-4).

Surely a person matters!

Leaving a Mark

During the months following my father's funeral, a thought began haunting me: Since home is neither a place nor a people, maybe it's a *persona*. Maybe my place of belonging can be found in the uniqueness that defines me. The accomplishments for which I am ultimately remembered. The proverbial, one-of-a-kind "empty place against the sky when my cedar falls."

After all, most of us spend a lifetime trying to build an identity that will matter, that will last. This partially explains why architects build, painters paint, and some of us write books: to define ourselves. To leave our mark. Maybe even to *find* ourselves.

Yet, in our prodigal attempts to find ourselves, we sometimes run away from our real identity—and from what matters most and lasts longest.

Jesus' most well-known story is about a young man who ran from himself in order to find himself. We call him the prodigal son.

Prodigal. The term fits my search too. Like the prodigal son, I left home young. Deliberately. Tried not to look back. Maybe in some twisted, adolescent way, I felt ashamed of the world of my roots. Like the prodigal, I felt restricted, maimed by a sense of limitedness, wanting something more expansive. It seemed to me then that everything in my childhood world was very humdrum. Confined. Pedestrian. I chafed to escape this "restrictive" identity.

So long before I physically left home, I had already left home a thousand times in fantasy. Seventeen miles to the south of our house, over rangeland of rough hills and brush coulees unmarked by roads, lay the Montana border—and a new country. The very word *south* seemed wild, intriguing, and mysterious, luring me like a siren call. I often dreamed of running away into the south hills, where I could hide among the trees and gullies in my own secret place. Maybe cross the border to Montana—even explore some of the exotic places "way down south," where life was surely a storybook of exciting adventure.

Then I left home physically. Left the homestead. Distanced myself from those good people—those "ordinary" and "boring" people, as they appeared to my adventurous adolescent eyes. And eventually I literally headed south, far beyond the hills that framed my childhood world, all the way to those storybook places I had imagined: Tennessee. There, far from my roots, I felt free to shape a new persona, to be a different me.

Of course, the old me tagged along. Everywhere I went. In the early stages of my academic career, I did very poorly, just as I had in high school, barely surviving academic probation. Consequently, Mondays through Fridays I still felt quite ordinary—and inadequate to boot.

But I lived for the weekends. On weekends I could escape into a less pedestrian identity. Within a hundred-mile radius of my college, scores of little country churches invited students to drive out on weekends to fill their pulpits. I immediately found these kind country folks enormously interesting, like characters from a Civil War novel. They spoke in such quaint and colorful metaphors. Their Southern ways were so different from the "ordinary" life I had known.

Besides, these good folks loved to encourage "preacher boys" like me. They made us feel useful. Special. They would listen to my sophomoric sermonizing as if in rapt attention. Afterward they would brag on my "talks" and say they were proud to have me as their "little preacher." Then these skilled Southern cooks would pile the country tables high with delicious foods—again, all new and exotic.

Oh yes, those weekends were something! On those days I

could put painful feelings about my unsophisticated persona and academic inadequacy out of mind. I could be a different person and feel the intoxicating sense of a fresh, new me emerging.

I guess I must have expected that my new persona would be visible and lasting; that it would be my place, my "home." So I became bent on leaving my mark.

Losing Touch

While I steadily lost touch with my roots, paradoxically, I still longed for what was best about them. That longing sometimes embellished my memories of home, touching up the family portrait with a gilded brush, until at times my idyllic fantasy scarcely resembled the actual, ordinary reality of my upbringing. So real did this fantasy become to me that when I actually, physically returned home for periodic visits, I felt incredible disappointment. I discovered—as most of us do—that family and old friends, reuniting after long separations from each other, simply pick up the story where it was left off. And we all place each other back in the roles where we "belong." These visits home shoved me back in touch with my ordinariness and with my fears of being stuck with it. And oh, how I needed to feel *extra*ordinary!

Gradually I became a multiple prodigal, internally and externally. A prodigal not just from a place. Not just from a people. I wandered away in my soul as well. With time I found myself very far from home in many of its best forms. Free of the old me, I would have said. Free of my ordinary self. Yet I actually came under bondage to freedom. Never content in any place. Always longing to get back home. But I had lost the map to get there.

The words of this old song described my struggle:

> Now the miles I put behind me
> Ain't as hard as the miles that lay ahead.
> And it's way too late to listen to
> The words of wisdom that my daddy said.
> The straight and narrow path he showed me
> Turned into a thousand winding roads.
> My footsteps carry me away,
> But in my mind I'm always going home.[3]

Soon Forgotten

It took me years to realize that "ordinary" is normal. That we are all ordinary. That God sometimes uses very ordinary persons for very extraordinary purposes.

What's more, even extraordinary accomplishments are soon forgotten, as this story from William Willimon drives home:

Traveling in the south of England, our car broke down. While we awaited repairs, I wandered through the yard of the village church. Eventually, I found myself in the cemetery surrounding the church. Over in one corner of the cemetery there was a beautiful, low brick wall enclosing fifty graves. The grass had nearly choked the plot. A large granite slab, set in the wall, bore the words WE SHALL NEVER FORGET YOUR SACRIFICE.

Here were fifty graves of young men. All around the ages of seventeen to twenty-five and all from New Zealand. Who were these men and why did they die here, in this little English village, so far from home?

There was no clue at the churchyard as to who they were or the circumstances of their deaths. I wandered down into the village. I found the town's museum and inquired there. The attendant at the museum told me, "Strange that you should ask. I have no idea, but given a few days I could certainly find out."

As I was not going to be there for a few days, I asked a couple of other people in town. No one knew. I surmised that they were soldiers who were stationed in this little town during World War I. Victims of the flu epidemic in 1918.

But no one knew. The impressive inscription in granite was a lie. We had forgotten their sacrifice. No one could remember.[4]

Surely Shakespeare was at least partly right when he wrote in *Julius Caesar*, "The evil that men do lives after them. The good is oft interred with their bones." Of course from heaven's perspective, nothing we do, from the smallest act of kindness to the most glorious accomplishment, is forgotten. God sees and remembers. But from a human perspective, our accomplishments—and even we ourselves as human characters—are quite quickly forgotten, usually long before our bones are interred. As the psalmist sadly sang, "Man is like a breath; his days are like a fleeting shadow" (Psalm 144:4).

On a flight from New York to San Francisco, my friend Chris overheard the conversation of a young couple sitting next to him. When the flight attendant brought the cold snacks, the couple opened the packages of Paul Newman mustard to spread on their sandwiches, and the young woman asked her husband, "Who is Paul Newman?"

"I'm not really sure," the husband responded. "He might have had something to do with Hollywood. But I think he is best known for his salad dressing."

So there, Ol' Blue Eyes. Welcome to the club of the quickly forgotten!

This "club" did not escape the notice of the ancient Hebrew poets:

> You turn men back to dust, saying,
> "Return to dust, O sons of men."
> For a thousand years in your sight
> are like a day that has just gone by,
> or like a watch in the night.
> You sweep men away in the sleep of death;

CHAPTER ELEVEN: MY PLACE IN THE SUN

they are like the new grass of the morning—

though in the morning it springs up new,

by evening it is dry and withered.

(PSALM 90:3–6)

The week I first wrote this page, Roy Rogers, "King of the Cowboys," rode into his final sunset. His death closed the gate on the golden era of the movie cowboy. In his day Roy Rogers, along with his wife, Dale Evans, starred in scores of movies and hundreds of radio westerns. He recorded numerous albums and was one of the founders of the globally famous four-part harmony group Sons of the Pioneers. For decades Roy Rogers and Dale Evans drew top box office. But on news of Rogers's death, a television reporter's random street interviews found few people who had even heard of him. In actual fact, Roy Rogers had ridden his last "happy trail" into the sunset—and out of the public eye—more than thirty years ago.

Fame simply does not last. Some young crowds don't even know who the Beatles were. And it won't be long before no one remembers Nicole Kidman, Alan Jackson, Julia Roberts, or George Clooney. Dare I say, someday even Elvis will be forgotten.

Death and decay and passing away are written on the winds of time. Shakespeare put it this way: "Tomorrow, and tomorrow, and tomorrow, creeps in this petty pace from day to day, to the last syllable of recorded time; and all our yesterdays have lighted fools the way to dusty death. Out, out, brief candle! Life's but a walking shadow, a poor player that struts and frets his hour upon the stage, and then is heard no more. It is a tale told by an idiot, full of sound and fury, signifying nothing."[5]

Carolyn and I lived in Abilene, Texas, for nearly twenty years, where I ministered in a large church. For fifteen years I spoke on daily radio in Abilene. I regularly addressed all sorts of civic events and graduations. My picture frequently appeared in the local newspaper and on television in those days.

We raised our family in Abilene—four children, one from kindergarten through college. I baptized, married, and buried scores of people there. But just last spring, on a return visit to Abilene, I walked into the offices of my old church, whistling and waiting to see heads pop out of office doors to greet me. But—would you believe it?—I had to check out several different offices before anyone even knew me!

Ancient Scripture is right on point: "There is no remembrance of men of old, and even those who are yet to come will not be remembered by those who follow" (Ecclesiastes 1:11).

In 1996 James Van Tholen, then thirty-one, and his wife, Rachel, moved to Rochester, New York, where Jim became pastor of a Christian Reformed church. Jim's ministry quickly endeared him to his people. But then the unthinkable happened: Early in 1998, malignancy struck and spread quickly to the length of Jim's spine. From March until October, Jim struggled through treatments that promised no cure. On

October 18 he summoned enough strength to preach his final sermon, which included these haunting words:

> I've been thinking what it will mean to die. The same friends I enjoy now will get together a year, and three years, and twenty years from now, and I will not be there, not even in the conversation. Life will go on. In this church you will call a new minister . . . and eventually I'll fade from your memory. I understand. The same thing has happened to my own memories of others. When I mentioned this to a friend, he reminded me of those poignant words in Psalm 103:15-16: "As for man, his days are like grass, he flourishes like a flower of the field; the wind blows over it and it is gone, and its place remembers it no more."

For the first time, I felt those words in my gut; I understood that my place would know me no more.

In his poem *Adjusting to the Light*, Miller Williams explores the sense of awkwardness among Lazarus's friends just after Jesus has resuscitated him. Four days after his death, Lazarus returns to the land of the living and finds that people have moved on from him. Now they have to scramble to fit him back in:

> *Lazarus, listen, we have things to tell you.*
> *We killed the sheep you meant to take to market.*
> *We couldn't keep the old dog, either. He minded you.*
> *The rest of us he barked at.*

Rebecca, who cried two days,

Has given her hand to the sandal-maker's son.

Please understand—we didn't know that Jesus could do this.

We're glad you're back. But give us time to think.

Imagine our surprise. . . .

We want to say we're sorry for all of that.

And one thing more.

We threw away the lyre.

But listen, we'll pay whatever the sheep was worth.

The dog, too.

And put your room the way it was before.

Miller Williams has it just right. After only a few days, Lazarus's place knew him no more. Before cancer, I liked William's poem, but now I'm *living* it. Believe me: Hope doesn't lie in our legacy; it doesn't lie in our longevity; it doesn't lie in our personality or our career or our politics or our children or, heaven knows, our goodness.[6]

Amen, Jim.

Legacy and career rarely last. Nor do visibility and influence. "The paths of glory lead but to the grave," wrote the eighteenth-century poet Thomas Gray.

A wise ancient put it this way: "Don't be impressed with those who get rich and pile up fame and fortune. They can't take it with them; fame and fortune all get left behind. Just when they think they've arrived and folks praise them because they've made good, they enter the family burial plot where they'll never see sunshine again. We aren't immortal. We don't last long. Like our dogs, we age and weaken. And die" (Psalm 49:16-20 MSG).

It Won't Get Us Home

Even if we should be one of those rare persons who become visible and stay remembered, leaving our mark on history will not make us feel at home.

To a few people, it might appear that I have left somewhat of a mark. At least among some professional peers, I enjoy a small degree of visibility at the moment. But in reality, not that many people are impressed. Certainly not my kids! In fact, to my surprise, I am not as impressed with myself as I thought I would be.

Of course, in the small picture, I enjoy the affection and feel thankful for the mildly visible role I play in my little world. But in the largest picture, this visibility leaves me both disillusioned and profoundly unsatisfied—in part because I know deep down that whatever positive reputation I enjoy is based mostly on illusion. (The folks who affirm me surely must not know my darkest side.) And even if some of the "positive press" were partly true, still it has not taken this prodigal home— *because it cannot.* Affirmation and visibility can't take anyone home. Not me, and not any of the sons and daughters of the human family. Because home is not a persona!

Being awarded places of honor among human beings does not tell us who our Father is. Or *where* He is. And being regarded by people as successful does not take us home. Henri Nouwen said it for us: "In every satisfaction, there is an awareness of limitations. . . . Behind every smile, there is a tear. In every embrace, there is loneliness. In every friendship, distance. And in all forms of light, there is the knowledge of surrounding darkness."[7]

You can mark it down in ink: Home is not a place. Home is not a people. And home is not a persona, a profile, or a mark left on history.

Friend Moses, you seem never to have been an ambitious career-builder, driven to leave your mark. On the contrary, the Bible says, "Now Moses was a very humble man, more humble than anyone else on the face of the earth" (Numbers 12:3). Clearly compassion, not ambition, is what motivated you. You "watched them at their hard labor" (Exodus 2:11). And your heart heard the call of God. Oh no, Moses, your story tells me that if you were moved by any personal interest at all, it was not lust for headlines, but longing for a homeland.

Goodness knows your position in the Egyptian royal family would have assured you a high-profile persona. But you exchanged that place of power for solidarity with slaves. You even accepted leadership reluctantly! "Who am I, that I should go to Pharaoh and bring the Israelites out of Egypt?" you said (Exodus 3:11). And in the end, you gracefully handed your leadership position over to another.

Moses, it is obvious that you did not expect a sense of personal significance to be your homeland. You knew what we all must learn: Visible profiles don't last, and accomplishments won't ultimately fulfill. You knew that what we're really looking for is something infinitely larger and more meaningful than our faces on Mount Rushmore. You knew that this hunger for someone to know us, for someone to remember our name, can only be satisfied by God himself.

Called by Name

Oh no. Our God is not merely an impersonal force standing behind a cold, mechanical universe. He is a father. As Jack Hayford reminds us, the Almighty "keeps galaxies spinning and worlds from falling out of orbit as they continue their trek through the vastness of space; yet He tended to my intra-uterine development (Psalm 139:13–16) and knows the number of the hairs on my head (Matthew 10:30)."[8]

The one who overrules the governments of the world, who limits the boundaries of the seas, is a Father who calls his children by name: "Adam, where are you?" "Moses, take off your shoes." "Samuel . . . oh Saaam-u-el . . . "

Oh yes, Cathy, someone knows your name. You will not be forgotten. Your place in history may be forgotten, but your name is now on the Father's lips—and it will be remembered forever.

PART FOUR: IN ALL THE WRONG PLACES

Shuswap Lake, B.C., July 18, 1988, 5 a.m.

First thing this morning I read Psalm 39:4-6:

Show me, O LORD, my life's end and the number of my days;

let me know how fleeting is my life.

You have made my days a mere handbreadth;

the span of my years is as nothing before you.

Each man's life is but a breath.

Man is a mere phantom as he goes to and fro.

Almost the moment I read the words, nature conspires with Scripture: The sun peeks over the mountains above the narrows and sends a shaft of gold some eight miles up the lake to touch the beach beneath my feet. In that path of gold, a fish turns in the soft ripples near shore, leaving his expanding circle behind him. But the circle vanishes within seconds, and I wonder, is this symbolic?

God is an overwhelming and never-ending shaft of golden light. My life and accomplishments may create only a brief circle of ripples, then sink into the sea of time and be forgotten. Obviously, then, what matters most are not my accomplishments, but rather becoming united with God and reflecting his glory in quiet circles around me. And he will expand the ripples as far as he wills.

But he has adopted me as his child—forever. And for that I say, hallelujah!

PART FIVE

HOMEWARD BOUND

Goin' home, I'm always goin' home inside.
There's an ache in my heart
That I can't bear.
Take me home, take my hand and lead me home
Oh Lord
I'm so broken up inside
I need to hide in your love, in your hand,
So take me home.

—ANNE HERRING

Far better is it to dare mighty things, to win glorious
triumphs even though checkered by failure, than to
rank with those poor spirits who neither enjoy
nor suffer much because they live in the gray
twilight that knows not victory nor defeat.

—THEODORE ROOSEVELT

There are a lot of folks who creep

Into the world to eat and sleep

And know no reason why they are born,

Save only to consume the corn,

Devour the cattle, bread, and fish,

And leave behind an empty dish

And if their tombstones, when they die

Were not to flatter nor to lie

There's nothing better can be said

Than that they've eaten up their bread

Drunk up their drink . . .

. . . and gone to bed.

—AUTHOR UNKNOWN

He was born a man and died a grocer.

—SINCLAIR LEWIS

CHAPTER TWELVE

ON THE ROAD HOME: HIS PURPOSES

You can't go home again. . . .

You can't go back home to your family, back home to your childhood, back home to romantic love, back home to a young man's dream of glory and fame, back home to exile . . . back home to lyricism . . . back home to aestheticism . . . back home to the ivory tower, back home to places in the country . . . back home to the father you have lost and have been looking for, back home to someone who can help you, save you, ease the burden for you, back home to the old forms and systems of things which once seemed everlasting but which are changing all the time—back home to the escapes of Time and Memory.[1]

So wrote Thomas Wolfe.

Oh yes, yes, Mr. Wolfe, most human experience would say that you were right. My own experience too. Like you and millions of other rootless souls, I have tried—often—to go back to some homes that you can't get back to.

But there is another side to the story. Actually, I have come to believe that Wolfe was both right and wrong. He was right if you think of home the way he was thinking of it. But there is a sense in which Thomas Wolfe was wrong. Home—*real* home—is not somewhere else, sometime back there, with some group of loved ones, that occasionally can be revisited. Nor is it a unique persona carved out by leaving a mark on history. Oh no.

Rather, home—*real* home—can be anywhere, any time. Home is not so much being *present somewhere* as it is a *presence* that can go with us *everywhere*. And yes, oh yes, it is still wonderfully possible to get back home again.

Finding and fitting into God's purposes sets us on the road.

What We're For

On Sarah's first day of school, her teacher said, "Sarah, please be sure to bring in a special paper tomorrow. It's called a birth certificate."

Eager to please, Sarah rushed home and stammered, "Mommy, my teacher wants me to bring a special piece of paper to school with me."

"And what piece of paper is that, Sarah?" Mother asked.

For the life of her, Sarah could not remember what to call the thing. "Mommy, she wants my—oh, you know—she wants to see my—*my excuse for being born!*"

Oh yes, Sarah. We all want one of those!

What *is* the purpose of being born? What is a person for? If forks are for eating, cars are for driving, violins are for music, then human beings are for—what?

Sometimes I ask students, "Why are you going to college?" Most reply something to the effect of, "To get job training."

"And why do you want a job?"

"To earn money."

"And why do you need money?"

"So I can pay my bills. Rent. Groceries. So I can have a place to sleep and something to eat."

"And why do you need rest and food?"

"So I have the energy to get up and go to work."

"And why do you need to get up and go to work?"

"So I can . . ." And on the cycle goes. You get up. Go to work. Earn money. Buy food. Pay rent. Eat. Sleep. Get up and go to work and repeat the cycle—again and again. Day after day. Month after month. Year after year. Until one day you slow down, stagger off the road, and die in the ditch like a dog.

As my friend Landon Sanders used to say, "That is obscene!"

Surely a person must be *for* more than that!

No wonder we are so troubled by the thought of death. The "death thought" lurks in our shadows. It haunts our dreams. It hovers over our conversations. It disturbs our internal peace. As Harry Emerson Fosdick observed, "The reason we make so much noise on New Year's Eve is to drown out the macabre sound of grass growing on our own graves."

I once heard Tony Campolo liken the death thought to a key on one instrument in an orchestra, stuck down and screaming its shrill note. At first we pay it little attention. Although we may notice it, it doesn't bother us much while the full orchestra is playing. But after the crescendo, as one by one each instrument dies away, that shrill note screams louder and louder until it fills the whole sky.

I have come to believe, however, that it is not the thought of dying that terrifies us so much as it is the thought that we might never *really live* first. That we will come to the end of life, having found it pointless. Never having had a sense of ultimate purpose. Never having been really alive.

Perhaps our longings for a homeland are really longings to fully experience purpose and meaning in life.

Dramatic Disappointment

One particular Sunday evening, our church drama team eloquently captured this human quest for purpose. The sanctuary went black. Then a single spotlight isolated a high-school girl lamenting to a friend, "Bummer. I'm stuck in high school. Same dumb teachers, boring classes, and nerdy boys. Rules all over the place. I'm barely existing. But one more year and I'm out of here. In college I will be free to start really living."

Darkness.

Then the spotlight picked up a college student. "Yuck," he said. "This place is a prison. Classes. Papers. Exams. Same dreary dorm room, smelly library, and airhead girls. If I can hang in just one more semester, I will be out in the real world. And then I'll be really living."

Blackout.

The spot focused next on a young couple listening to a baby crying and watching the clock. "Is this what life is supposed to be like?" the young mother said. "We are chained to this responsibility. No time for fun—even if we could afford it. I'm already hankering for the empty nest. Then we can begin to really live."

Darkness again.

The next person in the spotlight was a stressed-out midlifer. "I thought when our kids were gone, life would get simple," he groaned. "But I feel more pressure than ever. The job is too demanding and too uncertain. But one day Dorothy and I will be retired. Then we can start really living."

Darkness.

The final spotlight fell on a silver-haired retiree. "Son," he said, "I am proud of your successes. But mine mean nothing to me. Life has been nothing more than cycle after cycle of rat races. Oh yes, since retiring I don't feel any pressure to perform. But I have a lot of time to think—and I don't like what I'm thinking. I'm embarrassed, at my age, not to know what life is for. I've searched a lifetime, but frankly I still haven't the foggiest notion. My ticker is bad, and the doc says I'm likely to check out soon. So promise me one thing: If you find out what human existence is all about, please, *don't tell me.* Now that it's too late, I'd rather not know what I missed."

Then the final blackout.

This drama actually echoes the cry of an ancient teacher: "'Meaningless! Meaningless!' says the Teacher. 'Utterly meaningless!' . . . What does man gain from all his labor at which he toils under the sun? . . . There is no remembrance of men of old, and even those who are yet to come will not be remembered by those who follow'" (Ecclesiastes 1:2-3, 11).

Discovering the Ultimate

I remember meeting a real-life person who could have stepped straight out of this skit—or this passage from Ecclesiastes. It was on the platform in a public high school under the strangest of circumstances. The minister of the church where I was a guest speaker pitched me as some sort of "resource person" on whatever subject he thought might interest the various venues where he scheduled me to speak. So there I sat on a platform in front of several hundred high-school juniors and seniors, billed as a "resource person" on drug abuse.

Flanking me on the right was a pharmacist, with special expertise in "dangerous substances." Next sat an attorney who specialized in drug-related litigation. To my far left twitched a nervous high-school senior who said he had left the druggy crowd because of "convictions." Between us sat another senior who boasted of being a full player in the drug scene. This second teen—we'll call him Vinny—struck me as an unusually intelligent, loquacious, and witty young man. His one-liners kept the audience in stitches.

First the pharmacist spoke, rattling off a litany of damaging side effects from various illegal substances: loss of hair, flaky skin, liver damage, brain damage. But the kids looked bored. They had heard it all before. They would have checked out completely if it weren't for charismatic Vinny on my left, who kept lobbing hilarious scuds into the speaker's presentation.

Next the attorney stood and outlined the legal consequences for various substance-related offenses. Same result. Bored kids, except for Vinny's deadly one-liners.

My palms began to sweat and my pulse raced, knowing that I was supposed to speak next—as a "resource person." In reality, I had little idea what I was talking about. I didn't think an occasional shopping visit to a pharmacy qualified me for the role! Surely Vinny would humiliate me even worse than he did the first two speakers.

By the time my turn came, however, I realized that a lot had been said—but the real question had not been addressed. So I opened with a question for Vinny.

"It's obvious that you and the rest of the people here know very well *what* could happen to you if you mess around with these drugs," I said. "But we haven't heard much about the *why*.

"Vinny," I probed, "knowing all the potential physiological, psychological, and legal hazards that go with it, why would an intelligent fellow like yourself make drugs a lifestyle?"

Vinny eyed me as if I were a creature stepping out of a flying saucer from Mars and said, "Man, you are spaced out like Arizona! You really don't get it, do you? The reason I do drugs, man, is because it's the living end! Why it's, it's—it's *the ultimate purpose for being human!*"

Sometimes, it seems, God gives us just what we need when we need it.

"Vinny," I said, "I think you are on to something. Whatever is the 'ultimate purpose for being human' is what a person ought to do. We definitely don't want to stand in the wings of life with our hats in our hands and let the ultimate purpose for being human pass us by."

Then I said to the audience, "I agree with part of what Vinny is saying. Whether it's drugs, alcohol, sex, or kicking your grandmother's dog, don't let your parents or your pastor or the principal or the policeman talk you out of doing it, if—if indeed—it *really is* the ultimate purpose for being human."

Turning to Vinny, I continued, "Vinny, I think you have the right reason for doing this. But I think that you have settled for the wrong ultimate. For me, the ultimate purpose for being human isn't something you swallow or poke or smoke or sniff. It is someone you get to know—and his name is Jesus Christ."

Then to Vinny and the whole audience, I urged, "Let me encourage you not to dismiss Jesus out of hand without listening to the straight story. Don't let the propaganda against him be all you hear. Check out some original documents written by his friends, Matthew, Mark, Luke, and John. Then make your decision about Jesus. You may still reject him. But if you don't buy into Jesus, do yourself a favor and make sure you come up with an ultimate purpose for your life that is a whole lot better than Jesus—if you can."

What happened next I never would have predicted. The whole audience broke into loud, sustained applause! I couldn't believe my eyes and ears. I glanced over at the principal and saw him wiping tears off his face with a handkerchief. I suspected it wasn't because of his Christian sentiment. (He had led me to believe there wasn't a religious hair on his body.) Rather, I think just seeing the kids show interest in *anything* enough to applaud made the principal get emotional.

Of course, most of the students weren't saying, "I buy into Jesus. Sign me up!" Rather, I think their applause meant something like, "You have touched a real nerve here." In fact, a girl confirmed this when she came up to me after the session and said, "I have no idea what the purpose of my life is. I have at least average intelligence, but I am flunking. I'm not getting along with my parents. I'm abusing drugs and sleeping around, and I hate myself. I would give anything in the world to know what a person is for. Mom says the point is to marry well. Dad says it's about money. My teacher says it's grades. My friends say, 'Party down.' I have no idea who is right!"

At this point the attorney walked into the conversation and, ignoring the girl, said to me, "Well, fella, I must tell you, I'm an atheist. But I'm not going to knock what you said to those kids, because everybody needs a crutch of some kind."

Again, God supplied what I didn't have to meet the moment. "I certainly agree that we all need help, because we surely cannot stand on our own," I blurted out. "But sir, you have me curious about something. Could you tell me, what is *your* crutch?"

I honestly had not meant to put the man on the spot. But I doubt that a punch to his solar plexus would have shocked him more. His color rose. He looked down at his feet. Then he cleared his throat and replied with a hint of defensiveness, "All right, I'll tell you. OK." Pause. *"I stay really busy!"*

For a moment I felt as if we were standing with our toes over the edge of the Grand Canyon of this man's despair. He was an agent of the law; but if we are merely high-grade cellular matter, what difference does it make whether there is order in society? This man was fighting drugs; but if we are only sophisticated amoebae, what does it matter if we scramble our brains and shrivel our livers?

He responded, "I stay really busy," but what I heard beneath that phrase was, "I keep moving fast enough to keep the wind roaring loudly enough in my ears, so that I don't have to listen to those little voices on the inside of me asking the big questions: 'Why?' and 'What is a person for?'"

Permanent Purpose

Let me venture a hypothesis: There is a direct connection between feeling at home and knowing what we are for. *Finding God-given purpose* at least gets us on the road toward home.

So what is our God-given purpose? I am dead sure of very few things, but I think I know the answer to this question. The Westminster Confession distills it for us. The catechist is asked, "What is the chief end of man?" To which he or she is to respond, "It is the chief end of man to glorify God and enjoy him forever." This is profoundly true. It is true, however, not because it is in the Westminster Confession, but because it is in the Bible.

The Greeks in New Testament times emphasized important points by simple repetition. In this way Paul the apostle clearly underscored the core of human purpose by expressing it three times in one Greek sentence in Ephesians chapter 1. He declared that we are designed—and history was shaped—for one reason: God chose us "*to the praise of his glorious grace*," that we "might be for the *praise of his glory*" and be sealed with the Holy Spirit "*to the praise of his glory*" (Ephesians 1:6, 12, 14).

We are designed to glorify God and enjoy him forever. That, in brief, is God's purpose for us. And not just to *exist* forever. But to *love God* forever.

"Eternal life" means something more than simply living an incredibly long time. That word *eternal* does not refer primarily to how long we live, but how well. It is true, of course, that God offers life that lasts forever. But our purpose is to *enjoy* him forever; merely *living* forever isn't necessarily good news.

During a country revival, I was urged (as I am sure were the last several summer evangelists before me) to call on a local businessman. Every member of this man's family was a devout believer—all except the storekeeper himself, although out of courtesy he usually attended a night or two of the annual revival.

So I went calling.

"Good to see you at the revival last night," I began.

"Nice sermon, preacher," he responded without feeling.

After some awkward conversation, I came to my point. "You must be interested, or you wouldn't be at the revival," I observed, continuing, "but folks tell me you have never given your life to Christ."

"Why would I want to do that?" he answered in an even but crisp tone.

"Because Jesus is willing to forgive your sins—and give you—everlasting life," I stammered.

His response left me speechless.

"Everlasting life is what I definitely *don't* want," he declared. "Life is miserable. I hate my life. Are you telling me it would be some kind of reward to get stuck with it forever?"

A few years later, this man took his own life. He had no appetite for more quantity of a life without quality. Sadly, I had not helped him see that eternal life is more about the *essence* of life (quality) than about the *length* of existence (quantity). Eternal life is the kind of life that God, our heavenly Father, lives and gives to his children. Jesus called it abundant life (John 10:10).

Glorifying God and enjoying *this* kind of life is what a person is for.

But while it begins here, abundant life is not fully experienced in this world. It is only "shining ever brighter till the full light of day" (Proverbs 4:18). Gradually, across a life of faith, we get glimpses: Loneliness moves toward connectedness. Grace gradually swallows up guilt. Hope progressively dispels despair. A sense of meaning eventually overtakes feelings of futility.

Our pointlessness moves toward purpose as we begin to sense that we are part of something infinitely larger than ourselves. We begin to feel at home *in the purposes of God.*

Although they may be buried and almost hidden from our conscious memories, there lurk for most of us "God-memories" that whisper to us from the past. We may have long chosen to manage life on our own—even succeeded fairly well. We may have covered over the God-memories. Decided we've outgrown them. Yet the truth is, we can still revisit them and begin our journey home from their starting point. In fact, we must—if we are ever going to find the kind of flavor in life that we really want.

As Whittier penned it:

> We search the world for good. We cull
> the bright, the great, the beautiful.
> And weary seekers of the best,
> we come home laden from our quest,
> and find that all the sages said,
> was in the book our mothers read.[2]

Or in the immortal words of St. Augustine, "You have made us for yourself, O God, and restless are our souls until they rest in you."

Ah, friend Moses, in spite of being uprooted again and again and again, you were fully at home—because you fulfilled God's place, your destiny, in your time. You listened for his voice. You responded to his call. You paid the price, giving up power, prestige, wealth, and comfort; choosing instead "to be mistreated along with the people of God" (Hebrews 11:25).

And you taught me something of what it means to glorify God.

The moon has no glory of its own. But how beautifully it reflects the majestic glory of the sun into our dark world! Just so, friend Moses, you knew we human beings have no glory of our own. So you asked the Almighty, "Show me your glory" (Exodus 33:18).

He gave you indirect glimpses. And just these mere glimpses gloried up your face (Exodus 34:29) and sent your silver moonlight across our dark planet, softly reflecting the Father's glory—until the blazing light of Jesus came, changing us from one degree of glory to another into his likeness (2 Corinthians 3:18).

Your soft moonlight beckoned me to follow my real purpose—to glorify God and enjoy him forever. And because of that reflection, Moses, you helped set me on the road toward home.

I took a day to search for God,

I climbed the highest steeple

But God declared, "Go down again,

I live among the people."

—AUTHOR UNKNOWN

CHAPTER THIRTEEN

PARTWAY HOME: HIS PEOPLE

Dr. Scott Momaday, Regents' Professor of the Humanities at the University of Arizona, has known since childhood that he is an Indian. A story is told of his strange and touching journey back to his roots—and his identity. When Momaday was just a child on the Kiowa reservation, his father wakened him early one morning. "Son," his father said, "it's time to go. It's time to go."

"Sleepily I went with my father to the house of the 'old one,'" Momaday recalls. "My father left me there all day long."

The "old one" began to speak halting but spellbinding words to the boy, her tongue rich with the accents of the native peoples. She recited poems and chanted songs of the Kiowa. She told how the Kiowa had come from a hollow log in the Yellowstone River. How they became a growing tribe. She told of the Kiowa hunting buffalo. Fighting other tribes. Blizzards. The coming of the white man. She told of the disappearance of the buffalo, then the starvation. Moving south to Kansas, then Oklahoma. Finally, humiliation, deprivation. And Fort Sill.

The whole day long, Momaday listened to the "old one." Then, when the sky grew red in the west, Momaday's father returned and said, "Son, it's time to go." According to the story, this was a pivotal, defining day for Momaday. "When I arrived at the house of the 'old one' that day I was a lad," he said. "When I left I was a Kiowa."[1]

Scott Momaday knows who he is because he knows his story. He is a Kiowa. For him, home isn't a *place*; it is *joining the story of his people.*

Our Story

We believers have roots too. And a story that tells us who we are. Of course, that story runs back far beyond a hollow log in the Yellowstone River. The story begins with God himself. We are his children. He is our Father. We are "the people of his pasture, the flock under his care" (Psalm 95:7). From Adam to Abraham, our story unfolds. Then on to Moses and to David, then forward. Our story continues through the manger, up Calvary, through Easter and Pentecost, and across the centuries until this very day.

Ours is the story of a people.

Of course, God knows each of us privately and personally—even to the exact numbers of hairs on our heads (Matthew 10:30). He takes personal interest in us, even when we feel isolated from him and others. But God also knows we need much more than individual care. We do not flourish—don't even stay balanced—in isolation. So he keeps calling us together, drawing us out of our loneliness (at least *some* of it) and into circles of relationship. As the ancient Hebrew poet mused, "God sets the lonely in families" (Psalm 68:6).

J. C. Bailey was the first evangelist God used to prick my father's heart. After hearing Bailey preach, Dad wrote that evening to his girlfriend (who would later become his wife and my mother): "Dear Mary, tonight I heard Bailey teach from the Bible. He talked about the church. He said the church is not a building. It is not an organization, nor a denomination. But that in the Bible, the church is just a circle of believers gathered around Jesus!"

I love that word picture. Steve Smith does too.

"This Is for Us"

Steve Smith was only a child when the seed was planted. That was more than thirty years ago. Now, in addition to recruiting church-planting teams for the South Pacific area, Steve leads an exciting, growing young church in the northwest section of Sydney, Australia—along with Peter, Martin, Mario, and worship leader, Shep.

These five players on the Sydney leadership team have been "mates" for decades, some since childhood. They are men of prayer. Their money flows generously to the ministry. And the amount of time they pour into the life of this church—beyond their hours in the marketplace—is nothing short of astounding.

Best of all, they share a remarkable bond. Shep and Steve seem especially close. They have been fast friends since they were seven years old.

The seed was planted this way: Steve's house was next door to the church—which he and his family never attended. But then some church kids invited Steve to Bible camp, and he decided to go. The first day of camp, when he walked into his cabin and faced a room full of strangers, he was scared and already a bit homesick. And no one welcomed him—no one, that is, except Shep. Shep motioned Steve over to a corner, reached under his bunk, and pulled out a box that his mum had packed for him. Shep lifted the lid so Steve could feast his eyes on the dazzling contents.

Just last month Steve told me this story, and all these years later he still beams as he remembers, "The box was stuffed with biscuits and lollies" ("biscuits" being Aussie for cookies and "lollies" being Aussie for candy). Shep gave Steve a deep look into the box of camp treasures and then announced, "Steve, this is for us."

Those four words became the hallmark of their relationship across more than thirty-something years since: "This is for us." The words also describe the culture of the church that Steve, Martin, Peter, Mario, and Shep lead today. "We want to lift the lid to God's goodies for our community," Steve says, "and tell everyone inclusively, 'This is for us!'" "For us" was the seed that grew—and now defines a whole community of believers.

In fact, "This is for us" magnificently expresses God's heart. The Father, Son, and Holy Spirit long to share the rich and beautiful bond of loving community they enjoy in heaven. So Jesus showed up in our "cabin" with a treasure trove from beyond and said, "This is for us!" Jesus made this specific point in his parting prayer, when he prayed that "all of them may be one, Father, just as you are in me and I am in you. May they also be in us" (John 17:21).

And the gift goes on. What we have received from Jesus—the joy of fellowship with God and with each other—is too good to keep to ourselves. A frightened and homesick world so much needs the welcoming smile of churches that lift the lid to God's goodies and warmly announce the inclusive news, "This is for us!"

I know that in earlier chapters I contended that, ultimately, home is not a people. But there is a sense in which I must contradict myself. On the one hand, returning to my people—my physical kinfolks—will not get me home. But on the other hand, home *is* the presence of the people of God—God's "us"—at least temporarily and in part.

They Have a Name for It

When Fred Craddock was in seminary, he served for a short time as the minister of a small mission church in the Appalachians. A special tradition surrounded the mission's baptismal services on Easter sundown. They took the candidates out on a sand bar in the river and baptized them. Then they would climb out of the water and change into dry clothes in little tents on shore. In the gathering darkness, a sumptuous feast would follow; then all the folks would draw close around the fire and sing.

Craddock recalls what always happened next: "Glen Hickey—always Glen—introduced the new people. He gave their names, where they lived, and their work." As the ritual continued, the rest of the folks would circle tighter around. Then, in turn, each of the church members would speak up.

"My name is . . . and if you ever need somebody to do washing and ironing, call on me."

"My name is . . . and if you ever need somebody to chop wood, call on me."

"My name is . . . and if you ever need somebody to baby-sit, call on me."

One person after another would step forward and offer his or her special "gift" to the newly baptized.

"Finally," Craddock remembers, "Percy Miller, with thumbs in his bibbed overalls, would stand up and say, 'It's time to go.' And everybody left." One time, "Percy lingered behind, and with his big shoe kicked sand over the dying fire. . . . He saw me standing there, still. He looked at me and said, 'Craddock, folks don't ever get any closer than this.'"

"In that little community," Fred Craddock concludes, "they have a word for that—over in those hills of Tennessee. A special name for it. They call it 'church.' That's what they call it—*church!*"[2]

God's "us"!

God has set us in the "family"—the "church," the "called together," the "community of faith"—because we need each other. "None of us lives to himself alone, and none of us dies to himself alone" (Romans 14:7). We are checks and balances to each other. We learn from each other. We enrich each other. We grow each other. As Pastor Jack Hayford says, "In community, each of us can become so much more than we could ever become by ourselves. . . . The life of each believer is inextricably interwoven with the lives of the others. . . . If you try to avoid learning what God wants to do through those relationships, you withdraw at your own expense. You will be poorer for having done so."[3]

Forever Family

One summer in the midseventies, some Christians in south Florida invited me to join a number of students for an outreach campaign on the campus of the University of Miami. They wanted to target completely unchurched people, many of whom had sketchy, distorted, or even negative perceptions of words like *church, Jesus,* and *Bible.* So we carefully chose vocabulary that would not put off such people or send their minds down wrong thought-ways. For example, we spoke of Jesus as the "People Helper." The Bible was the "People Helper's handbook." And we referred to the church as the "forever family."

Each evening after the presentation, we broke into discussion groups, then ended with a question-and-answer session and refreshments. On the last evening, a woman we'll call "Roxie," fortyish and hardened looking, remarked, "I've never spent three evenings in a row with the same group of people, except to do drugs or have sex. And I sure haven't shared this kind of honest discussion about the meaning of my life before. I love this—but it will never happen again."

"Oh yes," we affirmed. "This could happen again—and again—for a lifetime." I explained how the forever family offered me belonging, no matter what city I was in.

"That's because you know people all over the country," Roxie challenged.

I assured her that in most cities I *didn't* know people. Yet with a phone call or two, I could connect with part of my "forever family."

Roxie reflected on this for long moments. Then she said, "I'd really like to be part of a 'forever family,' but I'm not sure I even believe in the 'People Helper.'" So in the weeks that followed, that south Florida forever family loved Roxie to faith in the People Helper—and last I heard, she was happily at home.

Moving to a New Home

M. J. is a physical therapist and enthusiastic Christ-follower—and was part of a church I once served. When he was in physical-therapy school, he struck up a strong friendship with a guy named Steve who wasn't sure he believed in anything very much. M. J. wanted Steve to know Jesus, but he never preached at him.

One fall day Steve and his wife, Mary, were moving to a new apartment and feeling overwhelmed by the mountain of boxes and furniture stacked everywhere. They couldn't believe their eyes when M. J. walked in, along with a dozen or more others— teens, young married couples, singles, and senior citizens.

M. J. made introductions: "Steve, meet my church. Church, meet my friend Steve." Then M. J. and "his church" jumped in and helped pack, move, and unload Steve and Mary's belongings in their new place.

Steve reflected later, "I had always thought of church as solemn cathedrals, long-faced people, and boring irrelevancies. But this picture of church was a totally new and irresistible idea." Before long Steve became an enthusiastic Christ-follower himself. Mary's journey took longer, however.

When Steve and Mary's first baby came just before Christmas, they invited Carolyn and me to their home for dinner and some "faith talk." As we sat beside their Christmas tree eating dessert, Mary confided that she really loved the sense of community in our church—how the young parents lived life together, even co-parenting each other's children; the way the church seemed to affirm and celebrate family. "I want to be part of a community like that," she said. "But honestly, I don't know if I even believe in God."

We assured Mary that she was welcome to join us on the journey of faith—that we were not going to pressure her about honest doubts. More than a year later, when Mary was pregnant with their second child, her heart finally "went over the bar," and she too became a follower of Christ.

Life looks very different for Steve and Mary since they found their home—their place among the people of God—ten years ago.

Oh yes, we can get home. *Home is among the people of God.* At least we can get some sense of home there—the shadowy hints of home.

Back to My People

The spring after Dad died, I made my first visit back to my people. I went back to speak to an annual gathering of churches from all over the area where I had grown up. That weekend I saw people I had loved since childhood but had not seen for decades. Several had been in my parents' "circle of believers" since long before I was born. One older lady reminded me that "aside from your own mother, I was the first one to change your diapers!"

I got at least partway home that weekend back in Saskatchewan. No, not merely by reconnecting with people who had known and loved me all my life. That was, of course, wonderful, and defining in its own way. But in an infinitely larger sense, these faces from childhood put me back in touch with the most important and anchoring of all human relationships. I rediscovered in a fresh way my sense of home *among the people of God.*

Real estate, family, and position won't last; they will leave or be forgotten. But the people of God have been around since long before you or I came on the scene, and they will go on forever.

Of course, the individual persons among the people of God keep changing. Even congregations are born and then die. But the church doesn't go away. As Jesus said, "The gates of Hades shall not prevail against it" (Matthew 16:18 NKJV). We are at home in the family of God as nearly as we are able to be at home at all in this world. We share the same family story with these, our people.

As I have often heard my friend Dr. Royce Money, president of Abilene Christian University, say, "A church is more like a family than anything else."

This is true, even though the people in our communities of faith may not always be the healthiest or most balanced of folks.

The poet of the Twenty-third Psalm wrote that the good shepherd "prepare[s] a table before [us] in the presence of [our] enemies" (v. 5). Mealtime in ancient Israel held enormous significance. By sitting at the table with someone, you implied acceptance of that person—so you had best give careful thought to the people with whom you sat down to eat! One obvious place the forever family "sits down to eat" is at the

Lord's Supper. But to the communion table, as to the table in Psalm 23, God sometimes brings a few of our "enemies."

You may have noticed that not every person in the church is pleasant to be around. Yet God delights in seeing us eat together in fellowship and peace—as family. In a gathering of believers, we share life alongside people we may not fancy being around under any other circumstance. Yet we have been joined together with them in unity by the Holy Spirit (Ephesians 4:2-6). Paul had this in mind when he said, "Accept one another, then"—in spite of differences, preferences, or the fact that you might not like each other all that much!—"just as Christ accepted you, in order to bring praise to God" (Romans 15:7).

Yes, being enwrapped in the arms of the people of God, our "forever family," takes us home. Yet still this "at home-ness" is only on one level—and by no means the deepest level. We are at home in a good sense, but not the best sense. For even here, among the people of God, we still feel a certain homesickness. Even around the Communion table, we long for something more. Jack Hayford identifies it: "We anticipate the ultimate 'last' Last Supper—the Messianic banquet that we will enjoy not in holy isolation, but in the heavenly, joyous presence of our Savior and the saved of all ages!"[4]

An old-time gospel song gathers up this kind of home-longing:

I've a home prepared where the saints abide,

Just over in the glory land

And I long to be by my Savior's side

Just over in the glory land.[5]

More Than a List

In the last chapter of his letter to the Roman church, Paul left us with, of all things, a long list of names. However, as Fred Craddock reminds us, we had better not let Paul hear us calling it "just a list." These were warm, flesh-and-blood people with whom Paul had shared life. Paul's list is a "church directory" of his friends in the faith. We would no more call such a directory "just a list"—be it first century or twenty-first—than we would call the Vietnam Memorial Wall in Washington, D.C., "just a list."

Yes, the wall at the Vietnam Memorial is a list of names, all right. But it is infinitely more. I felt the flesh-and-blood impact of the wall the first minute I visited there. Among the first few names is Jon Anderson—the same name as my oldest son. As if my son's name could be there too.

I watched as people stepped reverently up to the wall and placed flowers in front of special columns of names. Fingers slid slowly down the granite and stopped suddenly at particular names. Tears gushed. I saw a woman lift her small child up to the wall to touch a name.

This wall of names is so much more than a list!

Like the apostle, each of us today has a "list" of certain special persons among the people of God. Familiar faces in our circle of believers. Persons who have significantly impacted our faith or mentored us in our spiritual growth. Special believers who pulled alongside you or me at a crucial or formative moment: A Sunday school teacher. A minister. A coach. A friend.

Craddock suggests a compelling project. "Do you have a name or two?" he asks. "Keep the list. For you, it's not just a list. In fact, the next time you move, keep that. Even if you have to leave your car, and your library, and your furniture, and your typewriter, and everything else, take that list with you. In fact, when your [life] has ended and you leave the earth, take it with you."[6]

One of these days, folks will hold a funeral in your honor. And as Fred Craddock pictures it, on the other side, when you approach the gates with your list in your hand, the scene will go something like this:

St. Peter is going to say, "Now, what do you have there?"

"Well, it's just some names."

"Well, let me see it."

"Well, this is just a group of people that, if it weren't for them, I'd have never made it."

"I want to see it."

Finally, you give the list to him and he smiles, "I know all of them. In fact, on my way here to the gate, I passed them. They were painting a great big sign to hang over the street, and it said, 'Welcome home.'"[7]

That's right. Welcome home!

The world is round, and the place which may seem like the end may also be the beginning.

—IVY BAKER PRIEST

CHAPTER FOURTEEN

JOURNAL ON GREEN GRASS

What anyone else should experience at the first visit to a parent's grave, I cannot say. But on my first visit to Mom and Dad's last resting place, I discovered a surprising serendipity: In a real sense, God gave back to me the parents I had lost. I lost them as blood kin. But I reconnected with them as part of my "forever family."

I sat a long time on the grass in the cemetery trying to take this all in. Then I opened my journal and wrote—slowly and hesitantly at first, then furiously putting down on paper, before I lost them, the thoughts that tumbled through my head:

Weyburn Cemetery, Saskatchewan, August 31, 1994

> *That cold winter day I drove away from Dad's funeral saying, "I don't think I ever want to come back here." Of course, that was grief and depression speaking. Short weeks later my heart began to say, "When the fields are green, I am going back to Saskatchewan, back to visit my parents' last resting place." Well, here I am.*

Their funerals fell some two years apart, but one simple
bronze plaque marks the place where Mom and Dad lie side by
side. Engraved on the plaque is a single wild rose, a fitting
symbol of the old homeplace south of McCord where Mom and
Dad began their life together. Springtime always flooded the
coulee around the old house with a profusion of wild roses.
Engraved beside the rose is one word: Anderson. Below that
word, on the left, I read: "Mary 1905-1988." And on the right:
"Lawrence 1905-1990." That is all. That is so much how they
lived. And how they died. Very simply—yet in many respects,
very extraordinarily.

Below the Surface

I am strangely troubled because I feel no discernible emotion.
Is this normal? Is it simply the work of time? Nearly four
years have now passed since Dad died. Six since Mom. Could
this lack of feeling, in reality, be fear of deep, hidden emo-
tions so profound and massive that surface expression might
trivialize them?

I hear the roar—the long, steady, eternal roar—of the huge,
gray grain elevator just across Highway 39. At Mother's inter-
ment that roar drowned out the words Dr. Dan Weib spoke at her
graveside. I resented that intrusive sound, which so rudely
reminded us that one person's life and death seem insignificant
as time and commerce march on.

Strangely, that elevator stood silent the day we buried Dad.

Not because time and commerce deemed him more important than Mom, but simply because Saskatchewan agriculture hibernates in the dead of winter. So bitter was the cold that we could not linger at Dad's grave. There was no interment service. We simply laid him on the lowering device, turned our frostbitten faces away—and walked out of the cemetery, leaving Dad's casket on the surface in the blizzard.

Actually, the elevator was not totally silent that day. It groaned—sort of a low muttering—perhaps in apology for so much past rudeness, so much disregard for grief and disrespect for the dead.

Does anyone really matter very much? Dad's dream of a newly married homesteader—a place of his own, where he could live out a lifetime—is long since split into the hands of several who don't remember him much and could care less. And Mom's dream, toward which she toiled for years—a cozy house surrounded by lush shrubs and radiant flowers—is now a home for pigeons and skunks, encircled by a patch of weeds and brush. Not one flower remains!

Invisible Legacy

Yet my mother and father leave behind a mighty legacy of intangibles—and not just for their children. For hundreds of people. They did leave the world a better place than they found it. The ruins of the old homestead, the roar of the elevators, the diminutive size of their grave marker—these do not by

155

any means tell the real story. The best stories are never told in tangibles. Loyalty is intangible. And perseverance. And honesty. And kindness, hospitality, generosity, optimism, encouragement. All these things spring from love—invisible at its roots, though so visible in its fruits. And faith cannot be seen, nor the holy and almighty God in whom we put our trust. Yet this intangible faith in a living and invisible God drives every visible thing of lasting worth.

Mary and Lawrence Anderson made an incredible difference. And no matter what else I come to believe, I cannot believe that difference will die. Mom and Dad's influence links up with that of Carolyn's grandparents and of her parents—and of Carolyn herself. Now I also see it blossoming again in our children—and budding in our grandchildren.

This morning the local radio station played a song that went, "Islands in the stream, that is what we are." Islands? No, never! Not Mom and Dad. Not me. No one. Each island is an outcropping of the whole. Every island jutting through the surface of the water is actually part of one planet. Just so, every believing person is a part of the everlasting community of faith. Each person is but one "breaking through" to the surface—one manifestation of the presence of God, who is "over all and through all and in all" (Ephesians 4:6).

My mother and father are not mere fragments of flesh that appeared for a few years and then vanished. They were—and are—part of an everlasting and universal whole.

As I sit here on the green grass with dry eyes and level emo-tions and ponder this obscure marker before me, somehow I feel that something larger is happening. Some huge transfers are being made—transfers I am not able to pinpoint now and may not be able to for years to come. Possibly my bewildering lack of emotion at the grave of my parents is not really that important. Ah yes, tears will come and go now and then across the years. But because no tears fall now, I need not fear that my children will shed no tears when they sit on the grass around my grave. Nor that no transference will be made then. Nor that I will be disconnected from the past or the future. And I need not fear that neither they nor I will not make a difference.

I went home to my parents in a different sense that day. Though I had lost Mary and Lawrence Anderson from among my people, I found them again as part of my "forever family"— the people of God.

Oh yes, in a partial and shadowy sense, *home is found in the presence of the people of God.*

But still not in the deepest, richest sense. No, in the fullest sense, home is not found in people, not even God's people.

It can only be found in God himself.

PART SIX

HOME AT LAST

He wanted nothing more than to take the place of the ragged son kneeling before the father, to bathe in the golden light, to feel the tender weight of the father's hands on his shoulders. He wanted nothing more than to go home—wherever that might be.

—HENRI NOUWEN

I will dwell in the house of the LORD forever.

—PSALM 23:6

Lord, you have been our dwelling place
throughout all generations.

—MOSES

CHAPTER FIFTEEN

FULLY HOME: HIS PRESENCE

My friend Blackwell called yesterday, and our conversation drifted to our work.

"I couldn't do what you do," he commended. "I am a homebody. But you thrive on travel."

Blackwell meant to encourage me, but I felt compelled to explain.

"I do get energy from being with people, Blacky. People-work is my passion. And that puts me on the road a lot these years. But please understand, I genuinely despise the travel itself."

I am way past weary of airports and hotels and eating by myself. In strange cities. In strange countries. Among strangers. Feeling homesick. Alone.

But the truth is, we believers—even homebodies like Blackwell—are *always* away from home. Not just in foreign places or strange cities or impersonal hotel rooms far from familiar faces. Rather, from before the days of Moses until now, the people of God have never had an abiding place in this world. In one chapter alone, the Bible names Moses and fifteen other famous heroes of faith, then anonymously lumps in dozens more and concludes that they all have one thing in common: They all died away from home.

"All these people were still living by faith when they died. They did not receive the things promised. . . . And they admitted that they were aliens and strangers on earth. People who say such things show that they are looking for a country of their own" (Hebrews 11:13–14).

Like Moses and company and all believers since, I, too, ache to belong somewhere—and yet don't feel completely at home anywhere.

Moses, your story breaks my heart. You were born a stranger. And though you walked its palace halls for forty years, Egypt never was your homeland. Nor was Midian, where for forty more years, you followed flocks you didn't own across pastureland possessed by another. Then, for your last four long decades, you wandered a trackless and hostile "no man's land," utterly homeless.

Oh Moses, for a lifetime you longed for a homeland. And you came so close. But it was not to be. Your people finally wound up their wandering, crossed the Jordan, and settled in their long-awaited homeland. All of them.

All, that is, except for you, Moses.

You were left behind.

Alone.

Moses, did tears cloud your voice that day when you explained to your people, "The LORD . . . solemnly swore that I would not cross the Jordan and enter the good land the LORD your God is giving you as your inheritance. I will die in this land" (Deuteronomy 4:21–22)? Again and again, since my childhood, friend Moses, this final chapter of your story has left me with dark, heavy feelings. Your parting words to your people ached with painful sadness.

You seemed crushed at first. You even pointed the angry finger of blame at the people: "I pleaded with the LORD . . . 'Let me go over and see the good land.' . . . But because of you the LORD was angry with me and would not listen to me" (Deuteronomy 3:23–26).

Heaven would have none of your complaint, friend Moses. "'That is enough,' the LORD said. 'Do not speak to me anymore about this matter. Go up to the top of Pisgah and look . . . at the land with your own eyes, since you are not going to cross this Jordan'" (vv. 26–27).

Oh Moses, I so wish I could have struggled up the steeps of Nebo beside you on that final earthly pilgrimage: "Then Moses climbed Mount Nebo from the plains of Moab to the top of Pisgah, across from Jericho. There the LORD showed him the whole land" (Deuteronomy 34:1).

Moses, you stumbled alone up to that foreboding, lonely place. You reached the summit alone in the gathering gloom, and alone looked through a prism of tears at the homeland that would never bear your footprint. And in that final hour, you stood alone and homeless up on Moab's sad mountain as dark death mists closed around you.

Then the Lord said, "This is the land I promised. . . . I have let you see it with your eyes, but you will not cross over into it" (v. 4).

Joshua would lead the people in, while you, Moses, stayed behind. Excluded. Alone. Homeless. Your story sounds so heavily grief-laden and final. Your people thought so too: "The Israelites grieved for Moses in the plains of Moab thirty days, until the time of weeping and mourning was over" (v. 8).

Ah, but Moses, my friend and fellow wanderer, I am beginning to see that my dark twist on this tale is not the real truth of what happened on that mountain.

There is another way of seeing the Mount Nebo summit meeting. A very different way! Upon closer reading we find no hard evidence that Moses felt alone and sad. Note carefully: The ancient text does not say that Moses died in grief or with regrets. Nor does it picture a tragic demise. On the contrary, when we ponder the whole sweep of the Moses story, beginning to end, Mount Nebo actually becomes triumph, not tragedy.

No Longer Strangers

After all, this was no meeting of strangers. Moses and the High King of Heaven had been on intimate terms for more than forty years by this time. And God had watched over him many long years before Moses was even aware of it. When he was a baby lying among the bulrushes by the river, the hand of God rocked his basket-cradle. While his regal sandals strutted the princely palaces of Egyptian power, God paced invisibly beside him. Even when Moses struck down the Egyptian and fled familiar faces for fear of his life, God followed him. Watching. Waiting.

Then came that day on Jethro's grazing land, when God revealed himself to Moses, face to face and unmistakably. The voice of God from that burning bush broke the desert silence: "Moses, kick off your sandals and wriggle your toes in the dirt, because the land on which you are standing is holy ground." At that moment the pasture was not the land of Jethro; it was the land of God. Holy ground!

What made that ground holy? *God was there!*

We, too, can stand on holy ground. When we stand in the presence of the Almighty, the song voices it well:

> *This is holy ground—we're standing on holy ground,*
> *For the Lord is present, and where He is, is holy.*[1]

Thus Moses and his heavenly Father began their long journey together. From the burning bush on, they spoke often and intimately. Sometimes Moses encountered the Almighty on smoking, quaking, roaring Mount Sinai (Exodus 19:16–19). Other times, Moses visited with the Father in that special meeting tent outside the camp of the wandering Israelites, where God would talk to him "as a man speaks with his friend"

(Exodus 33:11). Still other times they conversed in thick darkness (Deuteronomy 4:11; 5:23).

Yet in spite of all his meetings with Almighty God, Moses longed for something more. "Show me your glory," he once begged. And God told him then, "You cannot see my face, for no one may see me and live" (Exodus 33:20).

Now years later, on the crest of Mount Nebo, it seemed that God was about to grant Moses his request. By this time the two were definitely not strangers. Moses was on a strange mountain, to be sure. Yet he was in a completely familiar place. For Moses was present with God—once more on holy ground.

If indeed Moses shed any tears that day, they must have been tears of relief and reunion. The wandering was over. He was home. Though he had often descended from mountaintop encounters with the Almighty, he would never again have to leave the presence of God.

At a hundred and twenty years of age, Moses retained his youthful vigor as he stood on Mount Nebo that day, pondering homelands. His eye held the same eagle glance before which proud Pharaoh had cowered forty years earlier. As T. B. Larimore phrased it, he was "a youth of one hundred and twenty summers, standing there with the world spread out beneath his feet. What unutterable thoughts were his as he looked upon that scene."[2]

Far away at the head of the Jordan, veiled in misty clouds, stood grand old Hermon, like a sentinel keeping watch across the centuries over this land flowing with milk and honey. To the south glittered the briny waters of the Dead Sea. At Moses' feet the rolling Jordan carried the snows of Hermon toward that salty destination. Beyond the Jordan lay beautiful Canaan, with her undulating hills, lush green fields, and streamlets flashing back the rays of the sun.

Moses took it all in. But he did not feel left out!

Here on the mountain, Moses stood much more solidly on the promised homeland than would those who settled on the real estate beyond the river. Canaan's land was not Moses' homeland. Oh no. For Moses actually stood on homeland right there on Mount Nebo.

Home before Heaven

But notice: Moses had not yet gone to heaven.

Don't mistake heaven for our homeland! Heaven would not be a homeland if it were not for God being there. I sometimes hear believers say, "My main goal in life is to go to heaven when I die." Of course, there is nothing wrong with wanting to go to heaven. I do. I have no other plans. But heaven is a by-product, not a goal. In fact, there is a way of desiring heaven that is actually selfish: "I'll get my skinny little backside through the pearly gates, devil take the hindmost." This desire may not be so much an eagerness for God as it is a greed for ultimate gratification. (Maybe it is even slightly akin to what might well have gone through the minds of the 9/11 terrorists as they slammed the airliners into the World Trade Center, confident that they would be instantly in a heaven where they would feast on rich foods and willing virgins.)

We don't get home by going *through the pearly gates*, but by coming *into the presence of God*. And if I don't enjoy the presence of God in the here and now—don't long to "gaze upon the beauty of the LORD," to "seek his face" (Psalm 27:4, 8)—then heaven will be a drag when I get there!

To illustrate: I married Carolyn because I wanted *Carolyn*. Not to get a house she would bring to the marriage. The reward of marrying her was to have more of *her,* not to share in her possessions. Similarly, Moses knew that the reward for seeking God is not a *place*, but a *presence*. The reward for serving God is *more of God himself.* And long before he went to heaven, Moses was in God's presence—face to face with the Father—feasting on the glory of God.

Undertaker from Above

The Bible tells us, "And Moses the servant of the LORD died there in Moab, as the LORD had said. He buried him in Moab, in the valley opposite Beth Peor, but to this day no one knows where his grave is" (Deuteronomy 34:5-6).

T. B. Larimore described this scene a century ago:

While [Moses'] soul was filled with rapture at this, the most sublime sight ever granted to mortal vision, the hand of God was laid upon the heart of that youth of one hundred

168

and twenty summers, that heart was stilled, and Moses was no more. No pain, no fever, no agony, no fear in dying, no struggle . . . his soul is filled, his eye is satisfied—and without a moment's warning the summons comes, and he falls asleep without a quiver, without a murmur.

He has the towering mountain for his couch, the bending heavens for his shroud, and the Lord Almighty for his companion . . . and God himself buried Moses in some lonely spot, unmarked, unknown, that his tomb might never be desecrated; that his lonely body might sleep there in solemn silence till the trump of God shall sound.[3]

Poets also pay tribute to this poignant passing:

> *By Nebo's lonely mountain,*
> *On this side Jordan's wave,*
> *In a vale in the land of Moab,*
> *There lies a lonely grave;*
> *And no man knows that sepulcher,*
> *And no man saw it e'er,*
> *For the angels of God upturned the sod,*
> *And laid the dead man there.[4]*

Moses was not left out. Moses wasn't homeless. Nor was he alone. Moses was with his Father! Oh yes. Rather than dying the lonely death of the homeless, Moses simply fell asleep, safe in his Father's arms. Where else in the universe could a person be more at home?

My little friend David Vanderpool III understands about home. His parents have taught him to love prayer. Regularly they join their hands around the table to pray. But once during prayer time, David's parents noticed that he had withdrawn his hand from their grasp. Sneaking a peek, they saw that he had raised his hands above his head, his little fists clenched as though grasping something.

When the prayer ended, David's mom asked him, "What were you doing with your hands over your head like that when we were praying?"

"Oh *that*," the boy responded. "I was holding hands with God."

Yes, David. How appropriate for those who feel at home with the Lord!

Home is where God is. So when we are with God, we are home. Now—and in heaven too.

Home at last. Home at last. Thank God Almighty, we are home at last!

*One thing I ask of the L*ORD*, this is what I seek:*

*that I may dwell in the house of the L*ORD *all the days of my life,*

*to gaze upon the beauty of the L*ORD *and to seek him in his temple.*

For in the day of trouble he will keep me safe in his dwelling.

—PSALM 27:4-5

CHAPTER SIXTEEN

HOME IS WHERE GOD IS

Dr. Fred Craddock, Emory University professor, tells this story:

When I was in graduate school, for three years I took courses
from Rabbi Silverman. Marvelous teacher. In three years he
never said the name "God." Do you know why the rabbis do
not say the name "God"? It's too holy! Three years, never said
the name "God." One day I asked, "Rabbi, I know you don't
say the name of God, but what is your favorite word to use
for God?"

"Oh," he said, "my favorite word [for deity]—my favorite
word—is *The Place!*"

The Place.

It is one of our oldest names for the Holy One. The Place.
God is The Place![1]

Where Is Home?

At one time it may have seemed to Moses that his home was a
physical place. First Egypt. Then Midian. Then it was to have

been Canaan. But in reality, it was none of these locations. By the time Moses died in the arms of his Father, he had long since learned that home was not a physical *place*—not even God's promised Canaan land

He had also learned that home was not a *people*. During early childhood Moses may have felt that the Egyptians were his people. But somewhere along the line, he began to sense his Hebrew-ness; and after killing the Egyptian, he threw in his lot with his blood kin.

Clearly the Egyptians were not his people. Nor were the Midianites, even though he married one. Yet, in the end, even his own Hebrew people left him behind. By this time, however, intimacy with his Father had come to be a more meaningful "place" than identity with his own blood family.

Nor was home a *persona* to Moses. As a prince of Egypt, Moses held fame and power in his hand. Yet apparently he lost interest in leaving his mark. He was a reluctant leader, recruited only at the insistence of the Almighty. And he seemed to have no inkling of the impact his persona would make on subsequent history. If any streak of ambition followed him across the wilderness, none of it climbed Mount Nebo with him. Moses' place, his home, was not a persona. Rather, he found his true sense of significance only in his Father's eyes.

Moses had come to see that home is not *a land*, but *a Lord*.

Not *ground*, but *God*.

Not *real estate*, but *a relationship*.

A place in God's presence.

God himself was Moses' homeland.

And he is ours as well.

God Is Our Homeland

Scripture writes this large. We sometimes sing the song, "The steadfast love of the Lord never ceases," with its climactic refrain, "The Lord is my portion says my soul, therefore I will hope in him." These words come from Jeremiah in Lamentations 3:24. "Portion" speaks of the land portions allotted to the Israelite tribes as their dwelling places in the Promised Land. What Jeremiah was saying was this: "*The Lord* is my portion of land. He is the dwelling place allotted to me." In other words, "God is my homeland!" Moses actually *experienced* this long before Jeremiah *explained* it.

God Is Our Temple

But God is not only our homeland. Zoom in closer. According to Scripture, God is also our *place of worship*. A woman at a well asked Jesus for directions to the right place to worship God. "Our fathers worshiped on this mountain," she noted, "but you Jews claim that the place where we must worship is in Jerusalem" (John 4:20). Jesus proceeded to explain that worship is not about geographical location. "God is spirit," he said, and the place of worship is *anywhere* and at *any time* when *anyone* worships God authentically and spiritually (v. 24).

These words of Jesus underscore the claim of the ancient psalmist: "O God, you are more awesome than your holy places" (Psalm 68:35 NKJV). No question, the temple in Jerusalem was impressive. But that magnificent structure was nothing at all in comparison with God. His holy *presence* was—and is—infinitely more awesome than any mere holy *building*.

At times Scripture speaks of God's presence and his "house" as one and the same: "Blessed are those who dwell in your house; they are ever praising you. . . . Better is one day in your courts, than a thousand elsewhere; I would rather be a doorkeeper in the house of my God than dwell in the tents of the wicked" (Psalm 84: 4, 10). And again: "One thing I ask of the LORD, this is what I seek: that I may dwell in the house of the LORD all the days of my life, to gaze upon the beauty of the LORD and to seek him in his temple" (Psalm 27:4).

Yes, God is our temple—our place of worship!

God Is Our Home

But God is not only our homeland and our place of worship. Zoom in closer still: God is also our very *dwelling place*. Our *home*. This note rings throughout the ancient Hebrew songs: "Lord you have been our dwelling place throughout all generations" (Psalm 90:1). "If you make the Most High your dwelling—even the LORD, who is my refuge—then no harm will befall you, no disaster will come near your tent" (Psalm 91:9-10).

Just as we long to be home in the Father's house, so also

the Father longs for his children to come home. The heartbeat of this two-way home-longing is heard nowhere more clearly than in the poignant story we call "The Prodigal Son." This story is not so much about a boy gone bad as it is about the longings in the father's heart. When the son came to his senses, he realized that the only place he would find what he needed was in his father's house; so he turned his heart toward home. But the truth is, the father was waiting long before the son began turning.

As Buckner Fanning puts it,

An incredible paradox of our searching is that God was the first one to start searching for us. Christian faith is the only . . . religion in the world that has a seeking God. All the other religions . . . are trying to find their way to God. . . . How do you get there to him? How do you find out how to pacify him or bribe him? How can I get his unlisted number? Not realizing that he has already gotten our number and has started calling us long before we ever started to call him. He created within us the desire to respond to his call.[2]

The boy's homecoming was obviously not to the farm, but to the father. Moses saw this centuries before. By the time Moses reached Mount Nebo, he knew that God is our dwelling place—our home!

Return Invitation

We will never wander so far away that we cannot still come home to the Lord. One person who wandered far away from

God—so far that he reached the "far country" of adultery and murder—came home to his Father's loving arms and wrote, "The Lord is my shepherd," ending that Twenty-third Psalm with this assurance: "Surely your goodness and unfailing love will *pursue me* all the days of my life, and I will live in the house of the LORD forever" (Psalm 23:6 NLT).

God is always waiting—on the homeland, in his temple, at his house—to gather us into his arms and welcome us home. Don Francisco sings it,

> *I loved you long before the time your eyes*
>
> *first saw the day.*
>
> *And everything I've done*
>
> *has been to help you on the way*
>
> . . . .
>
> *Even though My Name's been spattered*
>
> *by the mire in which you lie,*
>
> *I'd take you back this instant*
>
> *If you'd turn to Me and cry.*
>
> *I don't care where you've been sleeping,*
>
> *I don't care who made your bed.*
>
> *I already gave My life to set you free;*
>
> *There's no sin you could imagine*
>
> *That is stronger than My love*
>
> *And it's all yours if you'll*
>
> *come home again to Me.*[3]

When I was a boy down in Texas,

I lived in a ranch on the plains

Where Daddy worked hard ropin' and brandin'

I knew each dogie by name.

At sundown he'd call in the cattle

He'd let that old yodel ring.

Sweeter a sound has never been found

Than Daddy when he'd start to sing.

I'd hear, "Come home, come home,

come home little dogies.

Come lay down your burdens

and rest for a while.

Come home. Come home.

The Father is waitin'

Come home ya little dogies, come home."

—GARY FORSYTHE

CHAPTER SEVENTEEN

LIFE IN THE FATHER'S HOUSE

When I took my son to a Christian camp some years back, I noticed that the backboard of the outdoor basketball goal was painted with a giant eyeball. Presumably this was meant as a reassuring reminder of God's watchful presence. It hinted at Psalm 139, which says in part: "Where can I go from your Spirit? Where can I flee from your presence?"

But in reality the staring eyeball did not seem reassuring. Rather, it glared down angrily and seemed to scream, "I'm watching you, boy. And don't you forget it. You might run, but you can't hide." The eyeball reminded me of a troubling song I often heard years ago in rural revivals, rendered at the top of the lungs, with plenty of foot-stomping rhythm:

> There's an all-seeing eye watching you,
> Watching you (stomp, stomp)
> Watching you (more stomp)
> There's an all-seeing eye watching you.

Terrible song. Left kids with nightmares. But surely psychiatrists loved it. The aftermath of those guilty revivals must have brought them windfalls of new clients!

Of course, there is an "all-seeing eye" in Psalm 139 all right. But it is not anything like the accusing eye staring out of that terrible song or glaring down from that painted backboard. On the contrary, the psalmist makes clear that he feels secure under the loving, attentive gaze of a protective heavenly Father who tenderly looks out for his children. God's watchful eye assures us of his pursuing love and care, no matter where we go.

Before His Eyes

Look more closely at the psalm. The cry, "Where can I go from your Spirit? Where can I flee from your presence?" (v. 7) is not a lament; it is a comforting declaration of God's constant and everpresent watch care. In heaven. In the depths of the sea. On the far shore too. Even when we hide in the dark of night, he sees us as bright as day. Besides, the psalmist says, "You know when I sit and when I rise. . . . You are familiar with all my ways. Before a word is on my tongue you know it completely, O LORD" (vv. 2–4).

For my sixtieth birthday, my oldest daughter, Michele, wrote me a song, explaining, "It traces my path with you, Dad, and with my heavenly Father as well." She sang of her understanding being awakened to the reality of a father who loves her beyond words:

When I was a child, my thoughts would run wild
Thinking who God might be.

An angry old guy up in the sky,

Keeping an eye on me.

There are years of a man and time turns his hand

And I groped in the dark toward the day.

Was God friend or foe? I didn't know

And I hoped he was looking away.

In the darkness I called and he answered,

Gave his life so that I could be free.

And he loves me so much; he loves me so much

He can't take his eyes off of me.[1]

This is the "all-seeing eye" of Psalm 139. Like the reassuring, protective eye of a parent by the swimming pool, constantly counting all the heads. Smiling at his children's pleasure. Oh yes! God watches constantly. He loves us so much that he cannot bear to take his eyes off us!

But the psalm goes further: God not only watches us, he also holds us in his hand. Everywhere and in everything, the psalmist says, "Your hand will guide me, your right hand will hold me fast" (v. 10). What's more, we are always on the Almighty's mind. Listen as the psalmist insists: "How precious are your thoughts about me, O God! They are innumerable! I can't even count them; they outnumber the grains of sand!" (vv. 17–18 NLT).

Go count, if you can, the grains in one handful of sand; one cubic foot of sand; one cubic yard. Now expand your count to include the sand from all the beaches and deserts on the planet. When you come up with a number for all those grains of sand, consider that the number of times God thinks of you is still greater! What is more, the thoughts he thinks about you are love thoughts: "For God so loved . . . that he gave . . ." (John 3:16).

On His Heart

How can we grasp his love for us?

My friend in Chicago was determined to build healthy self-esteem into his daughter. Even before she was born, he laid his hand on her mother's tummy and spoke words of blessing. When she was a baby, he held her in his arms and told her over and over again how much he loved her. When she was a toddler, he walked with her hand in hand and explained how precious she was to him. He often knelt by her bed at night and thanked God for the incredible woman she would one day become.

Well, one evening, when the daughter was about five years old, she sat on the arm of her daddy's chair, playing with his hair as he watched the news. The TV blared out the story of parents who had dropped their children off at some agency and left—and hadn't been heard from since. The little girl perked up, her eyes and ears glued to the TV set. To dispel the tension, her daddy nudged her in the ribs and playfully kidded, "Mom and I have been thinking about dropping *you* off at one of those places. What would you think about that?"

The little girl jumped down from his lap, wheeled around in front of him, jammed her hands on her hips, and said, "Oh Dad!" Pause. "You wouldn't last five minutes!"

Don't you love the story! This girl has her daddy's number. What does she have to fear? He is the one who passionately and irrationally loves her with abandon—and she knows it.

Ah, my friend, how many of us have God's number? Do we understand that he is irrationally in love with us? He passionately pursues a relationship with each of us. Even now it's as if his finger under your chin tips your face toward his eyes, and he says, "Would you just love me? What I want most is a loving, trusting relationship between you and me."

This is the kind of love that met Moses at the burning bush. Led him through the desert. Followed him up Mount Nebo. This is the love that drew Moses to his true homeland. Moses lived a lifetime under the watchful gaze of his Father. His life was in the Father's hands. He was constantly on the Father's mind. Then, in the end, Moses died in the arms of his loving Father: the only place humankind can be completely at home.

Those arms have room for us too.

> *O lonely grave in Moab's land!*
> *O dark Beth-peor's hill!*
> *Speak to these curious hearts of ours,*
> *And teach them to be still.*[2]

Sunset and evening star,
And one clear call for me!
And may there be no moaning of the bar,
When I put out to sea,

But such a tide as moving seems asleep,
Too full for sound or foam,
When that which drew from out the boundless deep
Turns again home.

—ALFRED, LORD TENNYSON

LOOKING BACK
FROM HOME

Let me set the record straight: I feel more at home these days than ever in my life.

Of course I still wonder who I am. Am I Swedish? German? Canadian? Or American?

I am all, yet none, of these.

But I am home.

No, I haven't found the place nor the people to get back to. Nor has my face been carved into Mount Rushmore.

Nevertheless, I feel at home.

And my "at home-ness" is not because I live with the woman I love, which I do. Nor is it because we enjoy our Texas Hill Country house, which we do; sometimes we even call this place home. Nor is it because family lives near, which some do. No, all these things are gifts of God's wonderful grace, for which I thank him daily.

But these blessings are not why I feel at home. Rather, the solid sense of "at home-ness" in my soul runs infinitely deeper and is far more fulfilling than can ever be found in an ethnic identity or piece of real estate or sense of accomplishment—or even the love of a soul-mate spouse.

Yes—I am at home.

I find home *in prospect* within the purposes of God— which have set my feet toward home.

I find home *in shadow existence* among the people of God—which gets me partway home.

However, I find *real* home, *lasting* home, home *in substance* in the presence of God—which brings me fully home.

Of course, this is nothing I have earned—only received as a gift of God's grace. To tweak John Newton's familiar line, "T'was grace that brought me safe thus far—and grace has led me home."

I was born to a Swedish father—physically. However, I have been "born again" to a heavenly Father—spiritually, through what Jesus did for me on the cross (1 Peter 1:3-4). Which means I am now a child of God (1 John 3:1). And, as the familiar Twenty-third Psalm assures me, my Father's "goodness and unfailing love will pursue me all the days of my life." What is more, I am welcome in my Father's presence and can actually "live in the house of the LORD forever" (v. 6 NLT).

Deed to My Homeland

Home is where God is. So—let me say it again—I feel at home these days. God my Father has promised that his presence will

188

always go with me. He is, according to Psalm 46:1, my "ever-present help." And he repeatedly declares, "I will never leave you or forsake you."

Jesus underscores the Father's promises too: "If anyone loves me . . . my Father will love him, and we will come to him and make our home with him." And Jesus makes his own promise as well: "I will not leave you as orphans; I will come to you." He even says his Spirit will "live with you and will be in you" (John 14:17–18, 23).

Best of all, God's presence is permanent, lasting through this lifetime and beyond: "I am with you always, to the very end of the age" (Matthew 28:20).

Oh yes, God keeps his promises. So I definitely feel at home.

Staying Put

That familiar Twenty-third Psalm ends with the bold assertion, "I will dwell in the house of the LORD forever." Listen: The psalmist is adamant. "I am staying in the house of the Lord," he insists. "I ain't leavin'. Period. The matter is settled!"

Me too, King David. I am determined not to depart from the premises.

I love the house of my God. It has been my home since I was a child. Although at times I have wandered. At times ignored his "right paths." Too often dishonored the family name. Not that my heart has been filled with moral or ethical rebellion—just that at times it has seemed icy cold, and I have screamed out at my heavenly Father. And as Philip Yancey said, "Returning home from a lustful escapade seems so much easier than returning home from a cold anger that has rooted itself in the deepest corners of my being."[1]

Other seasons I have neglected and even avoided intimacy with my Father and with his family. I have broken the house rules and—to my deep regret—I have oftentimes broken my Father's heart.

But this is my home.

My Father's face grows more unspeakably precious with each passing year. In fact, if I were to become convinced that there is no God in heaven, no shepherd on my path, and Jesus is only a hoax, I would surely be a lost soul! I think I would lose my mind. I might even lose my life.

However, I am not a lost soul. I am a found son. In my Father's house. Where I belong. I may mark up the walls, smudge up the windows, scar up the furniture, scuff up the rug, and leave the tracks of my folly in every room and the trash of my failures on every stair. But I ain't leavin'.

This is where I will stay.

Surely my Father's goodness and mercy will pursue me all the days of my life. And I will—*I definitely will*—dwell in the house of the Lord forever and ever and ever.

My friend, as you stare at the final lines of this book, you may feel far from home. But there is wonderful good news.

Believe me—I know. You need not always wander, homeless. Your Father is out on the streets looking for you! He has always dreamed of your homecoming day! Long ago he said, "At that time I will gather you; at that time I will bring you home" (Zephaniah 3:20).

Michael Card sings the words for him:

> *Though you are homeless*
> *Though you're alone*
> *I will be your home.*
> *Whatever's the matter*
> *Whatever's been done*
> *I will be your home.*
>
> *I will be your home.*
> *I will be your home.*
> *In this fearful, fallen place*
> *I will be your home.*[2]

Come home. You have been a long time gone.

NOTES

INTRODUCTION: A LONG LINE OF WANDERERS

1. Walt Whitman, "Facing West from California's Shores," *Leaves of Grass* (New York: Bantam Classics, 1983), 90.

2. Buckner Fanning, "A Planet of Searchers," Audiocassette, UpWords Ministry. Used by permission. All rights reserved.

CHAPTER TWO: THE IMMIGRANTS: A HOMELAND FOUND

1. *Ellis Island & Statue of Liberty Magazine* (American Park Network, Seventh Edition, 1997), 9, 43.

2. Ibid., 47–48.

3. Ibid., 50.

4. Libby Smith, "Stranger in a Strange Land," *Arkansas Democrat Gazette*, September 10, 2000, 4H.

5. Johan Bojer, *The Emigrants* (St. Paul: Minnesota Historical Society Press, 1991), 306.

CHAPTER THREE: THE OUT-WANDERERS

1. Alan Jay Lerner & Frederick Lowe, "Paint Your Wagon"

(New York: Chappell & Co. Inc., 1951). Permission pending.

2. Bojer, *Emigrants*, 92-93.

3. Joe Diffie, "Home," *Sixteen Biggest Hits* (Sony). Permission pending.

CHAPTER FOUR: SENTIMENTAL JOURNEY

Epigraph. "Sentimental Journey." Words and music by Bud Green, Les Brown & Ben Homer. © 1944 (Renewed) MORLEY MUSIC CO. All rights reserved. Used by permission.

CHAPTER FIVE: THE FIRST NATIONS PEOPLE: A HOMELAND LOST

1. Dominion of Canada. *Sessional Papers* #4, Fifth Session, Third Parliament, 1878, Vol. 5, Sitting Bull Commission, 47-52. Report of the Secretary of State, Canada, year ended December 31, 1877, 24.

2. Martin Garretson, *The American Bison* (New York Zoological Society, 1938), 128.

CHAPTER SIX: RUNNING FOR HOME

1. Dee Brown, *Bury My Heart at Wounded Knee* (New York: Henry Holt & Company, Inc., 1970), 285.

2. Ibid.

3. Thomas B. Marquis, *Wooden Leg: A Warrior Who Fought for Custer* (Lincoln: University of Nebraska Press, 1957), 205.

4. James McLaughlin, *My Friend the Indian* (Boston:

Houghton Mifflin, 1910), 168-69.

    5. Dominion of Canada. *Sessional Papers* #4, 24.

    6. Brown, *Bury My Heart,* 420.

    7. Ibid., 437–38.

CHAPTER SEVEN: DRIVEN FROM HOME

    1. Brown, *Bury My Heart,* 440.

    2. Ibid., 441.

    3. Correspondence and research materials courtesy of the Nebraska State Historical Society.

    4. Brown, *Bury My Heart,* 441.

    5. James McGregor, *The Wounded Knee Massacre from the Viewpoint of the Survivors* (Baltimore: Wirth Brothers, 1940), 105, 118, 134.

    6. Brown, *Bury My Heart,* 444.

    7. Ibid., 445.

CHAPTER EIGHT: ALIEN IN ALL PLACES

    1. Henri Nouwen, *Making All Things New* (San Francisco: Harper & Row, 1981), 51–53.

    2. Bojer, *Emigrants,* 351.

CHAPTER NINE: THE OLD HOMEPLACE

    1. *The Canadian Rancher* (Austin, Manitoba, Canada: Rural Route Videos).

CHAPTER TEN: THE FOLKS BACK HOME

1. Edgar A. Guest, "Home," *A Heap o' Livin'* (New York: Lighthouse Press, 1916).

2. Henri Nouwen, *Here and Now* (New York: The Crossroad Publishing Company, 1997), 124-25.

3. "Going Home." Words by Anne Herring. Copyright © Latter Rain Music (admin), (Milwaukee: Hal Leonard Corporation), EMI. All rights reserved. Used by permission.

CHAPTER ELEVEN: MY PLACE IN THE SUN

1. Jack Hayford, *The Heart of Praise* (Ventura, Calif.: Regal Books, 1992), 242.

2. Ibid.

3. Diffie, "Home."

4. William Willimon, "He Has Been Raised," *Wineskins Magazine*, January/February 1998, Vol. 4, Number 1, 24-26.

5. William Shakespeare, *MacBeth*, Act V, Scene V, Lines 17-28.

6. James Van Tholen, "Surprised by Death," *Christianity Today*, May 24, 1999, 57-59.

7. Henri Nouwen, *Making All Things New* (San Francisco: Harper & Row, 1981), 51-53.

8. Hayford, *Praise*, 242.

CHAPTER TWELVE: ON THE ROAD HOME: HIS PURPOSES

Epigraph. Herring, "Goin' Home."

1. Thomas Wolfe, *You Can't Go Home Again* (New York: Harper & Brothers, 1941), 706.

2. John Greenleaf Whittier, "Miriam," *"Miriam" and Other Poems* (Boston: Fields, Osgood & Co., 1871).

CHAPTER THIRTEEN: PARTWAY HOME: HIS PEOPLE

1. Harold Hazelip, "Generation to Generation: The Path of Faith," *Upreach Magazine*, Herald of Truth, January 3, 2000.

2. Fred Craddock, "When the Roll Is Called Down Here," Preaching Today Tape #159, http://www.preachingtodaysermons.com/, a service of Christianity Today International. Copyright Fred Craddock.

3. Hayford, *Praise,* 35.

4. Ibid., 39.

5. J. W. Acuff, "Just Over in the Gloryland." Public domain.

6. Craddock, "When the Roll."

7. Ibid.

CHAPTER FIFTEEN: FULLY HOME: HIS PRESENCE

1. "Holy Ground," Christopher Beatty (Nashville: Word Music, 1982).

2. F. D. Srygley, ed., *Letters and Sermons of T. B. Larimore* (Hollywood: The Old Paths Book, 1950), 394.

3. Ibid., 395.

4. Cecil Frances Alexander, "The Burial of Moses," *The Best*

Loved Poems of the American People, Hazel Felleman, comp. (New York: Doubleday, 1936).

CHAPTER SIXTEEN: HOME IS WHERE GOD IS

1. Fred Craddock, "The Place," 1990 Brown Lectures, First Presbyterian Church, Dallas, TX.

2. Fanning, "Planet."

3. Don Francisco, "I Don't Care Where You've Been Sleeping." © Copyright 1977 by New Pax Music Press (ASCAP). All rights reserved. Used by permission.

CHAPTER SEVENTEEN: LIFE IN THE FATHER'S HOUSE

Epigraph. "The Last Cattle Call." Words by Gary Forsythe. All rights reserved. Used by permission.

1. Michele English, unpublished song, copyright 1996, written for my sixtieth birthday gift and recorded accompanied by her husband, Wes English. Printed with permission.

2. Alexander, "Moses."

EPILOGUE: LOOKING BACK FROM HOME

1. Yancy, *Soul Survivor,* 297.

2. Michael Card, "I Will Bring You Home," from *The Word* (Brentwood, Tenn: The Sparrow Corporation, 1992). All rights reserved. Used by permission.

LYNN ANDERSON

After spending most of his life ministering in churches, Lynn Anderson currently serves as founding president of Hope Network Ministries. Lynn's time is spend mentoring and equipping church leaders, conducting seminars nationwide, and writing books—including *They Smell Like Sheep; In Search of Wonder;* and *If I Really Believe, Why Do I Have These Doubts?* In 1990 he received his doctor of ministry degree from Abilene Christian University. He is a contributing editor to *Wineskins* magazine and advisory council of *Leadership.* His writing has been published in many other periodicals, including *21st Century Christian, Christian Chronicle, Image* magazine, *Power for Today, Restoration Quarterly, Upreach* magazine and *Leaven.* Lynn and his wife, Carolyn, live in San Antonio, Texas. They are the parents of four grown children and the grandparents of eight wonderful grandchildren.

Other Books by
LYNN ANDERSON

The Shepherd's Song-Take an adventure through the perilous and provocative life of David and learn how his struggles intersect your own and how his victories empower you to conquer your own giants.

If I Really Believe, Why Do I Have These Doubts?-There are times in every believer's life when the inevitable question arises: If I really believe, why do I have these doubts? This book is the first step to overcoming doubts and breaking through the obstacles of faith.

In Search of Wonder-Come join these seven searchers of the Word as they leave pointless issues behind, boldly seek God's Word, and find the true nature of genuine worship.

Navigating the Winds of Change-Learn how your church can manage cultural change without compromising eternal truths.

They Smell Like Sheep-Shepherding like Jesus means getting up close and personal with His people. Anderson's biblical approach to spiritual leadership delivers a powerful portrait of Jesus' leadership style and how we can emulate it today.

The Jesus Touch-Based on Jesus' "creative encounters" with the people He met throughout the Gospel of John, this powerful book will teach you how to treat each individual you meet with the creativity and love exhibited by the Master.

JOURNAL

Use these pages to document your own
homesickness and your journey toward home.

_____

_____

_____

_____

_____

_____

_____

_____

_____

_____

_____

_____

_____

_____

_____

_____

_____

_____

_____

JOURNAL

JOURNAL

JOURNAL